THESE FACTS WILL BLOW YOUR MIND!

FOR MY DAD, WHO NEVER TIRED OF
ANSWERING MY QUESTIONS.

AND FOR ISAAC—NEVER STOP ASKING THEM.

—EMILY

BLOOMSBURY CHILDREN'S BOOKS
Bloomsbury Publishing Inc., part of Bloomsbury Publishing Plc
1385 Broadway, New York, NY 10018

BLOOMSBURY, BLOOMSBURY CHILDREN'S BOOKS, and the Diana logo
are trademarks of Bloomsbury Publishing Plc

First published in Great Britain as *Brain-fizzing Facts* in August 2019 by Bloomsbury Publishing Plc
Published in the United States of America in November 2020 by Bloomsbury Children's Books

Bloomsbury books may be purchased for business or promotional use. For information on bulk
purchases please contact Macmillan Corporate and Premium Sales Department at
specialmarkets@macmillan.com

Library of Congress Cataloging-in-Publication Data
available upon request
ISBN 978-1-5476-0452-4 (hardcover)

Printed in China by C&C Offset Printing Co., Ltd., Shenzhen, Guangdong
4 6 8 10 9 7 5 3

To find out more about our authors and books visit www.bloomsbury.com
and sign up for our newsletters.

WHAT BREATHES THROUGH ITS BUTT?

Mind-Blowing Science Questions Answered

DR. EMILY GROSSMAN

ILLUSTRATED BY ALICE BOWSHER

BLOOMSBURY
CHILDREN'S BOOKS

NEW YORK LONDON OXFORD NEW DELHI SYDNEY

CONTENTS

SCIENCE is AWESOME!

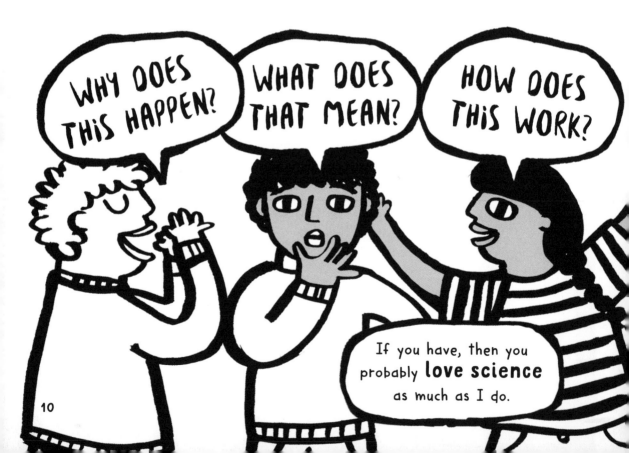

Hi, I'm **Dr. Emily** and **I love science!** Because science is about making sense of what's going on in the world around us.

When I was growing up, my **favorite** word was **"Why?"** I was constantly asking **questions**. I wouldn't accept anything anyone told me . . . unless they could give me an explanation. I used to drive my parents and teachers totally **bonkers!**

One study says that the average child asks **73** questions a day. How many do **YOU** ask? Have you ever asked something like . . .

> WHY DOES THIS HAPPEN?

> WHAT DOES THAT MEAN?

> HOW DOES THIS WORK?

If you have, then you probably **love science** as much as I do.

My favorite feeling is that
light-bulb moment
"Ohh!"
when suddenly everything makes **sense**.

I wrote this book because I wanted to share with you some
of my most **favorite weird** facts about **science**.
There are some **strange** and **amazing** things that happen in
the world around us. You'll find them here in the form of **30**
mind-bending questions, each with four possible answers.

But here's the **important** part:
as you read each question, see if you can **figure out**
the answer. I don't just mean which one is right,
but think about **why** it might be true.

Ask yourself . . .

Which answer makes the most **sense**?
Which answer is definitely **not** true?
Why might **this one** happen?
How might **that one** work?

If you don't know the answer, just take a guess. Please don't worry if you get it wrong. Some of the **best discoveries** in science came about when people got stuff wrong, made mistakes, or messed up their experiments. Do you know about Alexander Fleming?

Alexander Fleming was doing an experiment on **bacteria** when he made a **mistake**. The story goes that he left his dish of bacteria next to an open window and . . . went on vacation. The thing is, the dish also contained food for the bacteria, and if you leave food by an open window, what happens?

When Fleming got back from his vacation he realized his mistake. **Oops!** I'm sure he was pretty annoyed with himself. But instead of giving up and chucking the moldy dish away, he took a second look at it. And then he probably said something that is one of the most **important phrases in science**.

YEP. IT GETS MOLDY.

NO, IT WASN'T "EUREKA!" THAT WAS OLD ARCHIMEDES. FLEMING SAID, "OH! THAT'S FUNNY!"

What Fleming found so funny was that around the fluffy bits of mold on the dish, the bacteria had **died**. Fleming and his pals went on to isolate a chemical from the mold that could kill bacteria. They called it **penicillin** and it was the first **antibiotic**. Penicillin went on to save **millions** of **lives**.

So go on, take a stab at answering the first question. And don't worry if you get it wrong. Getting things wrong is the best way to **learn** and **progress**. First, try figuring out the answer yourself. Then you can see if my **explanation** makes sense. And then maybe **you'll** feel that light-bulb moment too.

DR. EMILY XX

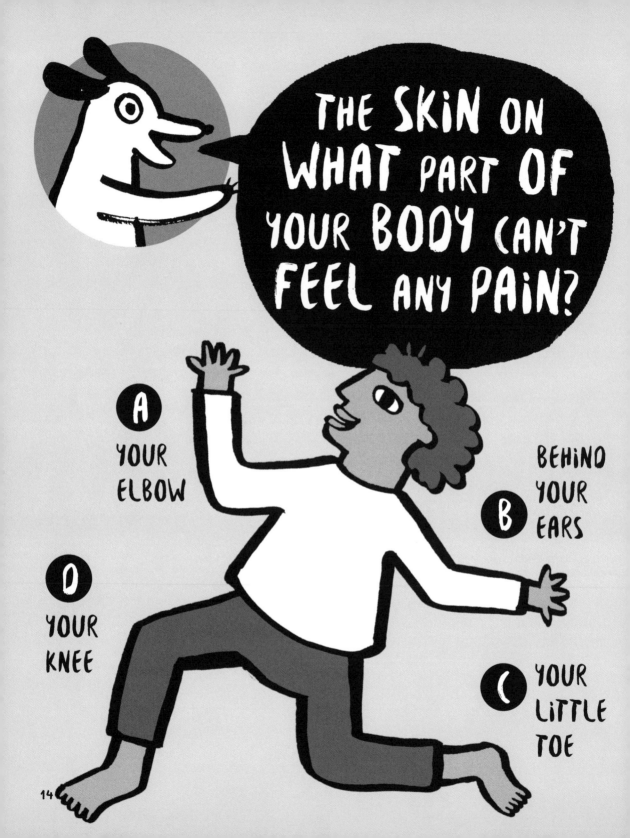

Pain is your brain's way of warning you that something is wrong, so that you protect that part of your body from further damage.

Pain is detected by **receptors** on your skin, which send electrical signals to your brain along long fibers called **nerves**.

The skin on the end of your **elbow**, called the **wenis**, is so thick and tough that it contains practically no nerve endings or pain receptors. So you can **pinch** your mom's elbow-skin as hard as you like and she will hardly feel it!

In fact, your elbow skin has so few **sensations** that if someone licked it (not that anyone would) you wouldn't even be able to **feel it** ...

Let a dog **lick** your elbow while you look the other way. It might be a bit **odd** but do it—in the name of science. Can you tell when they're licking you? Probably not!

Now try sneaking a peek at your elbow **while** it's being **licked**. This time you may **feel like** you can feel it. You can't actually feel anything different from before but your brain kind of fills in the gap. How cool is that?

THE **ANSWER** is **A**
THE SKIN ON YOUR ELBOW CAN'T FEEL ANY PAIN

Speaking of pain, next time you hurt yourself (somewhere other than your elbow skin), here's a **sneaky tip** for you:

It may sound a bit **strange**, but try looking at your bloody knee—or any other red or swollen part of your body—through the **wrong end** of a pair of **binoculars**. It will look **smaller** to you, so the damage to your body will appear to be less. This can sometimes **trick** your brain into sending you fewer pain signals.

Bizarrely, it might also hurt less if you're **not a redhead**. Scientists are currently arguing over this controversial topic, but some reckon that the same set of instructions (known as a **gene**) that causes some people to have red hair might also make redheads **more** sensitive to certain types of pain . . . and less tolerant of **cold weather!**

YOUR ELBOW SKIN MAY NOT FEEL MUCH PAIN, BUT ELBOWS CAN CERTAINLY FEEL RATHER FUNNY . . .

17

WHY IS YOUR ELBOW SOMETIMES CALLED YOUR FUNNY BONE?

A YOU CAN USE YOUR ELBOW TO TICKLE PEOPLE

B IT FEELS FUNNY WHEN YOU HIT YOUR ELBOW

C COURT JESTERS USED TO WAVE THEIR ELBOWS AROUND TO ENTERTAIN KINGS

D THE NAME OF THE BONE IN YOUR UPPER ARM SOUNDS FUNNY

AAARGH!

When you **bash** your funny bone it sure feels weird, right? It can send you **hopping** around the room making all sorts of strange noises.

When your sister jumps in the air yelling that you've hit her **funny bone**—while pulling a face that would appear to suggest that she's actually just been bitten on the butt by a **piranha**—what she **really** means is that you've **squished** a section of a **nerve** hiding inside her elbow.

THE FUNNY BONE'S GOT A SILLY NAME, AS IT ISN'T ACTUALLY A BONE AT ALL, IT'S A NERVE . . .

NERVES ARE LONG THIN FIBERS THAT ZAP MESSAGES TO AND FROM THE BRAIN, IN THE FORM OF ELECTRICAL SIGNALS. KINDA LIKE WIRES IN AN ELECTRICAL CIRCUIT.

The nerve inside your elbow is called the **ulnar nerve**, and it runs all the way down your arm and into your little fingers. The job of this nerve is to send **signals** from your **brain** to the **muscles** that move your fingers, and to send signals **back** to the brain telling it how your fingers **feel**. It works pretty hard when you're playing the piano. Or when your finger gets **nibbled** by a rabbit.

Like the other nerves in the body, the ulnar nerve is **protected** from the outside world, at least for **most** of its length, by layers of **bone** and **muscle**.

So you probably won't be able to feel it, even if you **push** quite hard on the skin of your forearm with something hard and pokey. Like a **carrot**.

But if you **straighten** your arm you might be able to feel that there's a little **gap** between the **knobbly** bits of bone on the underside of your elbow, **on the side closest to your body**.

CAN YOU FEEL iT?

Here, your nerve is only protected by your **skin**. So, if you bash your elbow in **just this very spot**, your poor **delicate** ulnar nerve gets temporarily **squashed** against the bones in your upper arm.

This can cause a **weird, tingly, numb** feeling in your little fingers, which might also feel a bit **painful**.

Some people think this **funny** feeling is how the funny bone got its **nickname**. This is probably true . . .

. . . but a more satisfying explanation is that the funny bone is also a **play on words**, because the technical name for the **bone in the upper arm** is . . . wait for it . . . the **humerus!**

HiLARiOUS, RiGHT?

THE **ANSWER** is <u>B</u>

YOUR ELBOW IS SOMETIMES CALLED YOUR FUNNY BONE BECAUSE IT FEELS FUNNY WHEN YOU HIT IT.

BUT THE BONE DOES SOUND FUNNY TOO!

By the way, did you know that your fingers don't actually contain any **muscles**? Don't **believe** me? **Try** leaning your right elbow on a table and **relaxing** your right hand, letting it hang down limply. Now, with your left hand **squeeze** the underside and topside of your right wrist **tightly** together. Did you see your fingers **curl in** slightly?

CREEPY OR WHAT?!

This is because you are pulling on bits of **cord**, called **tendons**, that connect your right finger bones to the **muscles** in your **lower arm** that operate your fingers— so this **draws your fingers in**, as if you were about to **grab** a monkey bar. Or a **banana**. Or a **pineapple** (well, maybe a small one). Or a . . . okay, I'll stop now.

BUT SPEAKING OF PINEAPPLES! . . .

WHAT CAN YOU DO TO MAKE A PINEAPPLE TASTE RIPER?

A STAND IT UPSIDE DOWN

B PLACE IT IN THE FRIDGE

C CUT IT OPEN

D SIT ON IT

HAVE YOU EVER WONDERED WHAT A PINEAPPLE PLANT LOOKS LIKE?

You might be surprised to discover that pineapples grow **upright**, instead of hanging down from a tree like apples and oranges.

Pineapple plants only produce one lonely pineapple each year, which sits proudly on a sort of **leafy perch** in the middle of the plant.

I'M ALL ALONE!

The **solitary** pineapple is connected to the rest of the plant by its **flat bottom**—not by the crazy **exploding** bit at the top that looks like a parakeet having a bad hair day.

This means that when the pineapple is picked, the bottom of the fruit (where it has been attached to the plant) is likely to be **sweeter, softer,** and **riper.**

Now, strictly speaking, a pineapple can't actually get any **riper** once it's been **picked.** But if you cut the top off and turn the rest of the pineapple **upside down** and leave it covered in foil in the fridge for a few days, the **yummy sugary juices** from the base will seep down through the pineapple, making it nice and sweet **throughout its length.** This should also prevent the **base** from starting to **rot** in its own sugary juices.

Here's another related **fruity fact** for you: there is a type of **strawberry** that tastes like . . . you guessed it, a pineapple. **Seriously.** These **undercover fruit agents** look pretty much like strawberries apart from the fact that they're bright **white** and have **red pips**. Perhaps more like strawberries who've gone out on a cold day without a sweater. But the **bonkers** thing is, according to some people, these weird **white** strawberries taste a bit like **pineapples**. So what do you reckon they're called? **Pineberries!**

Try and find some next time you're out shopping. Then **sneak** one of these double-crossing masters of disguise into your **gran's cereal** . . . and watch as she pulls a **funny face**.

TIME FOR **ANOTHER** EVEN **WEIRDER** FACT, FEATURING . . . YOURS TRULY, THE PINEAPPLE! BUT IS OUR PINEAPPLE FRIEND THE RIGHT ANSWER?

ABOUT HOW MUCH DOES THE WHOLE OF THE INTERNET WEIGH?

A NOTHING, SILLY

B AS MUCH AS A SMALL CRUMB OF BREAD

C AS MUCH AS A PINEAPPLE

D AS MUCH AS A SUBMARINE

You'd probably think that the **internet** doesn't weigh anything at all. It's not really a **"thing"** is it? It's more like a concept. **An idea.**

Actually, we can think of the internet as **information**. Information stored on **millions of computers** around the world. But information doesn't **weigh** anything, **right?** After all, your phone doesn't get any **heavier** the more silly cat photos you store on it, does it?

CUTE

WELL, ACTUALLY, THAT'S NOT QUITE TRUE.

27

YOU SEE, THE INTERNET STORES INFORMATION IN THE FORM OF BILLIONS OF TINY PARTICLES CALLED ELECTRONS.

These **electrons** are **captured** inside the electronics of our **phones** and **computers**. For example, storing a short **email** might involve around **2 billion electrons**. Now, if you've come across electrons before, you might be thinking—but electrons **weigh practically nothing**. Well, you'd be absolutely right. But the information stored on your computer or mobile phone doesn't change the actual **number** of electrons inside it. What it changes is how much **energy** each of these electrons has. Whether it is in a **high** or **low energy state**. **1** or **0**. Sort of like **up** or **down**. **Chocolate** or **vanilla**.

BUT COULD THIS MEAN THAT THERE'S ALSO A CHANGE IN WEIGHT?

Many many years ago a physicist called **Albert Einstein** came up with a really cool **equation** that links **energy** to **mass**. **Mass** is the amount of **stuff** something is made of, which also determines its **weight**.

Einstein's special equation **E=mc²** formed part of his **theory of special relativity** and is the basis of modern **physics**. You might have heard of it before—it's one of the most **famous** equations around. As equations go, it's quite a **celebrity**, actually. Truly. It even appears on **T-shirts**. And if it got married, it would probably feature in a magazine. Okay, sorry, I'll stop being **silly** now.

So here's the **cool** bit. Using this special equation, **physicists** realized that if information stored in computers and phones increases the **energy state** of these teeny tiny electrons, there must also be an increase in **mass**. And an increase in mass means an increase in **weight**.

IT'S ALL RELATIVE.

$E = MC^2$

In fact, using this clever method, it has been calculated that filling up a 4 GB Kindle device with digital books—that's around 2,000 books—would increase the weight of the Kindle by about a billion billionth of a gram. That's 0.000000000000000001 g—a ridiculously small increase in weight.

Such a tiny amount that even the most sensitive weighing scales would not detect it. But it is something. For the increase in weight to be as much as even the weight of a penny, you would need to fill up 3 billion billion Kindles. That's an awful lot of books. You'd never get through all of those over summer vacation. Even if they were good ones. Like Harry Potter.

Or this one, maybe . . .

But the **important** point here is that **information stored** by captured electrons **has weight**. And the information stored by the internet is an **awful lot more** than 3 billion billion Kindles' worth of books. In fact, in 2012, experts used these clever methods to calculate that **all the data** stored in the internet probably adds up to about **50 g**. That's the weight of a medium-size **egg**.

But since these calculations were carried out, the internet has been **growing** so **rapidly** that it's probably quite a bit **heavier** than that by now. We could **estimate** that it might by now be as heavy as something like . . . you guessed it . . . a **pineapple!** Although to be honest, no one really knows for sure.

THE ANSWER is C

THE INTERNET PROBABLY WEIGHS ROUGHLY AS MUCH AS A PINEAPPLE

Did you know that the world record for the **largest** pineapple is held by a **gardening granny** from the appropriately named Bakewell area of Australia? Her enormous pineapple measured 12 1/2 inches in length and weighed a whopping 18 pounds, which is about as heavy as a **Boston terrier** or **dachshund**.

Maybe she used it to make a pineapple pie. In which case, let's hope she **baked it well**. Get it? **Ha ha!**

Anyway, where was I before I started babbling on about pineapples?

OH YES, FUNNYBONES. OR INDEED, FUNNY FACTS ABOUT BONES . . .

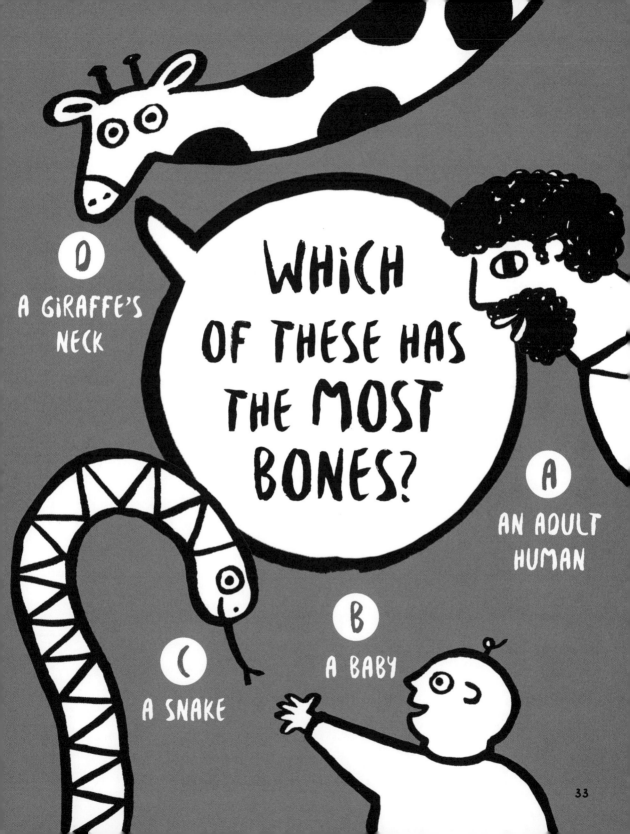

The human body can do a pretty **awesome** array of things—from climbing a mountain or doing a back flip to kicking a football or knitting a sweater. Tricky activities like these rely on the precisely coordinated action of over **200 bones** in your skeleton—206 to be precise—working together with your muscles, tendons, and ligaments.

The parts of your body containing the **most** bones are your hands—there are 27 bones in each one—as they have to do the **trickiest** and most **delicate** things, like making a Lego spaceship. In fact, more than half of the bones in your whole body are in your hands and feet.

You might be surprised to know that, despite its **ridiculous length**, a giraffe's neck contains the **same** number of bones as a human neck. It's just that each of the giraffe's neck bones is a lot **longer** than each of yours.

SO, AN ADULT HUMAN BODY DEFINITELY HAS MORE BONES THAN A GIRAFFE'S NECK.

What about a **baby**? A baby can't do half as many complicated things as children or adults can. Plus it's pretty **tiny**. So surely it can't have **more** bones than an adult? Bizarrely, it actually **can**. And it does. Quite a lot more.

Babies are born with between 275 and 300 bones and bendy bits of cartilage. Over time these will harden into bone. That's nearly **100 more bones** than the measly 206 that an adult human ends up with. So where do all the other bones go?

As the baby grows, groups of tiny bones and bits of cartilage **stick together**, or **fuse**, to form stronger, larger bones. A baby's **skull**, for example, is made up of five bone **fragments**, which slowly fuse together. That's why you should never push down on the **small soft spot** on the top of a baby's head. Here, the bones haven't yet fused, so there's only delicate skin and membranes covering the baby's **brain**.

THEY DON'T JUST FALL OUT OF A BABY'S EARS. DO THEY?!

All these extra bones and bits of bendy cartilage make a baby's body nice and **squishy** . . . so it can squeeze through its mother's birth canal when it's being born, and **bounce** when it falls on its butt.

So what about a **snake**? Snakes **slide** along the ground and **slither** up trees with extraordinary ease and precision. To help them achieve such effortless and highly controlled slithering, it is thought that some snakes contain **600 to 1200 bones!** This makes the snake the clear bone winner.

THE **ANSWER** is **C**

A SNAKE HAS THE MOST BONES.

READY FOR ONE MORE FAB FACT ABOUT BONES? OKAY THEN, HERE WE GO . . .

WHICH IS THE STRONGEST BONE IN THE HUMAN BODY?

 A THE JAWBONE

 B THE HIP BONE

 C THE THIGH BONE

 **D** THE LITTLE TOE BONE

If I ask you to think of a **strong material**, what pops into your mind? Probably something like metal? Or even concrete? All right, smarty-pants, **diamond** then. But not **bone**, right?

Bone may not **seem** like a particularly strong material, but would you believe it's actually **stronger** than both metal and concrete? "How much stronger?" I hear you cry. Well, seeing as you asked . . .

Gram for gram, bone is **stronger than steel**, and as for concrete . . . well, bone is not twice, not three times, but a staggering **four times stronger than concrete!**

Bone, like concrete, is what's called a **composite material**. This means it is made up of a **combination** of two quite different materials: hydroxylapatite (which contains lots of calcium), and a bendy substance called collagen. This super-powered combo makes bone mighty strong in **compression**— meaning you can **push down on it** pretty much as hard as you like, as long as you press **along the length** of the bone, and it's unlikely to break. However, if you were silly enough to hold a bone out **sideways** and whack it at 90 degrees, like a karate chop, it could easily **snap**.

This explains why you can **snap** a chicken bone in two with your bare hands. Unless of course you **soak it in vinegar** first, in which case it would go all **bendy**. Try it, it's weird. The acid in the vinegar dissolves away all the calcium, which is the stuff that makes the bone hard, leaving behind the **bendy collagen**.

Now, the **jawbone** is definitely **one of** the strongest bones in the body, but the absolute heaviest, longest, and strongest bone in the human body is the thigh bone, properly known as the **femur**. This makes sense, as your two femurs have to support the weight of pretty much your entire body. In fact it's been predicted that a **rhino femur** could hold a whopping 120 tons before snapping—that's more than the weight of **three heavy trucks**!

THE **ANSWER** is **C** THE STRONGEST BONE IN THE HUMAN BODY IS THE THIGH BONE.

So, while you should definitely avoid jumping off anything high onto a hard surface (like concrete), luckily most of your bones are pretty hard to break. Well, apart from the **teeny tiny ones in your little toes**, which are so delicate that it has been estimated that almost everyone has broken at least one in their life! Although they're not as tiny as the **tiniest bone in the body**, the u-shaped stirrup bone, or **stapes** (pronounced stay-peez), which is only one tenth of an inch long. Luckily it's tucked away safely inside your **inner ear**, where it helps transmit **sound waves** to your brain.

EVEN AMERICAN LEGEND EVEL KNIEVEL, WHO BROKE A RECORD-BREAKING 433 BONES DURING HIS CAREER AS A MOTORCYCLE LONG JUMPER, PROBABLY DIDN'T BREAK THAT ONE!

When it comes to things that, like bone, are strong in compression, the **last** thing you'd probably think of would be . . . **an egg**. After all, "walking on eggshells" means walking very **carefully** indeed. So eggs must be pretty **fragile**, right?

Not so fast. It turns out that **walking on eggs** is actually totally possible! In fact, you can **stand** on a carton of eggs and they won't break. Seriously. Try it—but **very gently**. And it's probably best to put some old newspaper underneath the box. And **check** with whoever bought the eggs . . . you know, just in case . . .

Eggs are **so strong** in compression that not only can you stand on them, but it's also virtually impossible to **crush** one in the palm of your hand—as long as you push on its **ends**. Try it.

The secret to an egg's strength is in its **shape.** Eggshells are **double-ended arches**, and arches are one of the strongest shapes known. Which is why **bridges** and **windows** are often designed in the shape of an arch. **But** . . . tap an egg sharply on its **side** . . . and voilà, you're ready to make an omelet. Right, before we move on, do you want to know some other **crazy** things you can do with an egg?

OH ALL RIGHT THEN, IF YOU INSIST . . .

DR. EMILY'S EGGCITING EGGSPERIMENTS

So eggs are super strong if you press on their ends, but **drop** one on the floor and it'll smash, right? **Not necessarily**.

You can actually make an egg **bounce**. Like a bouncy ball. Want to know **how**? I thought you might. All you have to do is soak the egg in a bowl of **vinegar**. Vinegar is an **acid** and it reacts with the **calcium carbonate** that makes up the eggshell, so the shell will start to **dissolve**. This is a **neutralization** reaction, which produces a salt, some water, and carbon dioxide gas—so you might see some **bubbles** forming.

After two to three days of soaking, rinse the egg and then very carefully **peel** the crumbly shell away. You'll be left with a raw egg, held within a thin transparent film called a **membrane**. You might even be able to see the yolk **floating** around inside. Rinse the egg **very gently** . . . and then you can try bouncing it. Even better, trick a friend by asking them to drop this weird-looking egg. Imagine their surprise when it **bounces!** Please do it very gently, though. And it's probably best to put some old towels down on the floor—if you drop it too hard, it could **burst** open and splatter raw egg over your mom's best rug. Nice. Don't say I didn't warn you. For a less **messy** but equally bouncy version of this eggsperiment, **hard-boil** the egg before soaking it in vinegar.

Here's another cool eggy thing you can do to impress your friends. Ask them if they can make an egg **jump**. Or more specifically, if they can **flip** an egg using a shot glass. (You'll need to ask an adult if you can borrow a shot glass.) Hang on, before you tell me that's **easy peasy** (if a little messy)—how about **without touching the shot glass?** Not so easy, right?

WRONG. ALL YOU HAVE TO DO IS BLOW ON IT. SERIOUSLY.

Draw a dot on one end of an egg using a felt pen, so you know which end is which. Then place the egg in the shot glass with the dotty end up, and put the glass on a nice hard surface.

Now, with your face just above the egg, **blow really hard** straight down onto the top of the egg in a sudden short sharp burst. Blowing makes the air above the egg **move really fast,** and this fast-moving air creates an area of **low pressure** above the egg.

The air trapped in the shot glass **below** the egg is still at normal pressure, which is now **slightly higher pressure** than the fast-moving low-pressure air **above** the egg. This **difference in pressure** will make the air under the egg try to **rush upward** out of the shot glass toward the area of low pressure, creating an **upward force** on the bottom of the egg. This force **pushes** the bottom of the egg up . . . and if you're lucky, the egg will **jump** out of the shot glass!

The air pushing upward on the bottom of the egg will probably be a bit **uneven** on each side of the tip, so it's quite likely that **one side** of the tip will experience slightly more force than the other. And lo and behold the egg might start to **rotate**. If you've managed to blow **hard enough** to produce a big enough upward force, as if by magic the egg will **flip around** . . . and land in the shot glass **upside down!** As if it's done a little eggy somersault.

This upward force that occurs when there is **lower pressure above an object than below it** is sometimes called **lift**. Lift is what allows airplanes to fly. You might have noticed that an airplane wing is **tilted slightly backward**. As the plane zooms through the sky at great speed, the **angle** of the wing causes the air hitting the underside of it to get all **bunched up**, increasing the **air pressure**, while the air rushing over the top of the wing **spreads out**, decreasing the pressure. This difference in pressure produces a force underneath the wing that **pushes upward on it**—just like the force that caused the egg to jump out of the shot glass. If the airplane is traveling fast enough, the **lift force** becomes greater than the **weight** of the plane—and hey presto, the airplane **lifts into the air**.

NOW, BACK TO EGGS . . . .

You can also do an awesome trick with an egg and a **milk bottle**. Or any kind of glass bottle really, as long as it has a neck that is **slightly too small** for an egg to fit through. Or at least that's what **you** think.

Hard-boil the egg and peel off the shell. Now place a little bit of **cooking oil** around the neck of the bottle so it's nice and **slippery**.

Making sure you're being supervised by a grown-up, take a small piece of **newspaper** and very carefully **light it** with a match and drop it into the glass bottle.

Immediately place the egg **over the mouth** of the bottle. It will rest there for a few seconds until the flame goes out and then . . . **shluppp** . . . the egg should pop right into the bottle! How on earth does this happen?!

You see, when the newspaper burns, the air in the bottle gets **hotter**—so the air particles gain more **energy** and start moving away from each other. This makes the air **expand** so it takes up more space. This means that some of the air has to **escape** from the bottle, by pushing around the edges of the egg resting on the neck of the bottle. But as soon as the flame goes out, the air inside the bottle cools down again and starts to **contract**. As the egg is sitting on the neck of the bottle, no air can get back into the bottle, so this creates a bit of **empty space** in the bottle—what we call a **partial vacuum**. This vacuum sucks on the slippery egg and **squeezes** it into the bottle. **Shluppp!**

49

THE **ANSWER** is **D**
AN EGG CAN'T DANCE.

So an egg can bounce, jump, and even sneak inside a milk bottle. Crazy. But did you know that an egg can also **count to ten**? Okay, that was a joke. Of course it can't. That would be just plain **silly**.

Now where was I before we went off on a **weird journey** all about eggs? Let me think . . . eggs . . . strong things . . . aha! Bones!

SO, WE ESTABLISHED THAT YOU'D FIND YOUR STRONGEST BONE IN YOUR THIGH, BUT WHERE DO YOU RECKON YOU'D FIND YOUR STRONGEST MUSCLE?

To be able to answer this question we really need to consider what we **mean** by **strongest.**

The job of a muscle is to **contract,** which means to shorten in length. Muscles do this in order to **pull** on our bones, or to make **squeezing** motions deep inside our bodies—like when our heart **pumps** or our intestines **squeeze food**.

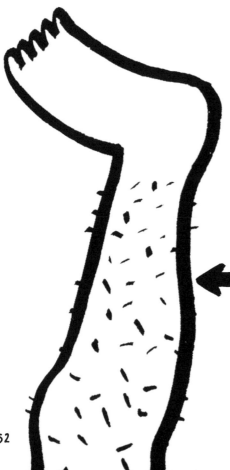

If we were looking for a muscle with the strongest **pulling power**, the champion puller would have to be the muscle running down the back of your lower leg, called the **soleus**. This muscle is working pretty much **all of the time** when you are on your feet, to stop you from **falling flat** on your face. Without your long-suffering soleus **constantly pulling on the bones** in your lower legs, every time you tried to stand up **gravity** would just pull you back down into a **crumpled heap** on the floor. That would be pretty **embarrassing** during morning assembly! The soleus muscle also helps you to walk, run . . . and dance around your living room like a loon.

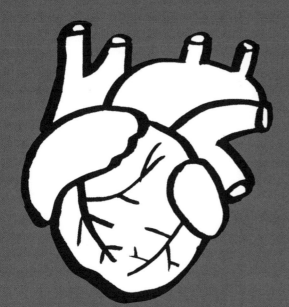

The **gluteus maximus** muscles in our butts, affectionately known as the **glutes** to their friends, are the **largest** muscles in our bodies . . . and they're pretty strong too. Our glutes help us jump over a stream, climb a tree, or chase a dog around the park. They're also needed to keep our upper bodies **upright**.

Now, if we were talking in terms of **hard-working muscles**, the winner would have to be the heart muscle—properly known as the **cardiac muscle**. This **turbo-charged** muscle keeps contracting day in, day out, pumping blood around your body. The average adult heart beats around 72 times each minute, which adds up to around 100,000 beats a day, over 3 million beats a year, and a whopping **2.5 billion beats over an average lifetime**—without ever getting tired or stopping for a rest and a cup of tea. That sounds like rather a lot of hard work to me.

Our **eye muscles** could be thought of as our **cleverest** muscles. When our heads are moving, the muscles around our eyes are constantly **adjusting** the position of our eyeballs, so that we can stay **focused** on a **fixed point**. Try it—stay **focused** on the words on this page but **move your head** around a bit. Your eye muscles are clever, aren't they?! In fact, if you were to keep reading this book for an hour (go on, you know you want to), your eye muscles would make around **10,000 coordinated movements.**

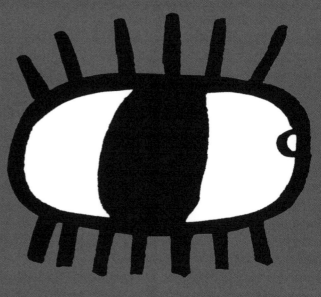

Unlike your relentless perky **heart muscles**, your eye muscles get **tired** after a while and need to take a break. That's one of the reasons we need to close our eyes every evening and get a good night's **sleep**. Having said that, your eye muscles do work pretty hard when you're **dreaming!**

A special mention must go to the **tongue** as a contender for the most **versatile** muscle—allowing us to do a whole **variety** of different things, like eat, talk, sing . . . and do tongue-twisters. Even when you're asleep, your tongue is constantly **pushing saliva** down your throat. Unless you're a pillow-dribbler.

But the prize for the **strongest** muscle in terms of **absolute** strength, meaning the maximum amount of **force** that the muscle can generate at any one time, would have to go to the **masseter** muscle in the **jaw.** Although the **uterus** is also a pretty strong contender—ask any woman who's been through childbirth. The muscles in the uterus have to **contract** pretty hard to push the baby out!

An **average adult jaw** can push down on food trapped between its back teeth, or **molars**, with a force of around **200 pounds per square inch (psi)**. That's like having a **small brown bear** sitting on your food.

THE **ANSWER** is **B** YOU WOULD FIND THE STRONGEST MUSCLE IN YOUR BODY IN YOUR JAW.

NO WONDER WE CAN CHEW ON SOME PRETTY TOUGH TOFFEE.

BUT THE STRENGTH OF THE HUMAN JAW IS NOTHING COMPARED TO SOME OF THESE FEARSOME CHOMPERS . . .

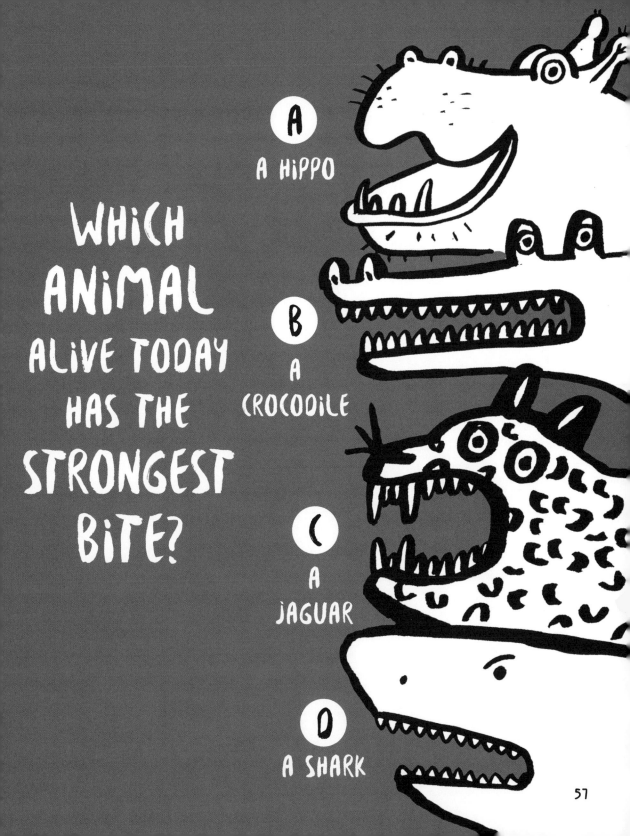

WHICH ANIMAL ALIVE TODAY HAS THE STRONGEST BITE?

A — A HIPPO

B — A CROCODILE

C — A JAGUAR

D — A SHARK

When it comes to bite strength, the **jaguar** is no pussycat. These formidable hunters have the strongest bite of **any cat**. Their awesome jaws can exert a force of up to **2,000 psi** on their prey—that's like the weight of **two small cars**. Their jaws clamp down almost twice as hard as the chomp of a **tiger**, and with almost **ten times** the average bite force of a **human** set of gnashers. With this ferocious bite they can **pierce the skulls** of their prey, which can include vicious alligators. Or even puncture the **crunchy shell** of a turtle.

I MUCH PREFER JUICY LEAVES.

Although not **quite** as powerful as a jaguar, gorillas have the strongest bite of all **primates**— a group of animals that includes apes, monkeys, and humans. So a big **silverback** can munch and grind on a variety of pretty **tough stuff**. Like . . . er . . . **tree bark**. Hang on. Tree bark? Who'd want to eat tree bark? It's not exactly a **delicacy**. Not that I'm about to say that to his face. He might get rather offended and decide to munch on **my arm** instead. Just for fun, of course, as gorillas are actually **herbivores** so they only eat plants. Except for the occasional **ant**.

Anyway, it just so happens that tree bark is packed full of **salt**, which gorillas need to eat to survive. So it turns out that those tree-munching gorillas are **pretty sensible**, actually. Perhaps they put it on their **chimps**! Ha ha. Get it? Put salt on their chimps? Like chips? Oh never mind.

If we expand our search to **all mammals**, there is really only one other animal that can compete with the awesome power of a jaguar's jaws, and that's the **hippopotamus**.

While our muddy friends might **look** cute, they are the **most dangerous** large land animals in Africa. Even though they don't actually eat meat, hippos are incredibly **aggressive** and often **attack with no warning**. So don't go wallowing in a hippo pond. Even if you're wearing boots.

What about **whales**? No, not the country, silly, that's Wales. I meant the big **fish-like mammals**. Whales certainly have really **large mouths**. In fact, the **bowhead whale** is thought to have the biggest mouth of all living creatures.

But the thing is, while whales may indeed have monstrous mouths, they don't really use them to **bite**. In fact, most of them don't have **teeth**. Their food just washes in through their big bristly jaws. This means their jaw muscles have not evolved to be very strong at all.

What about if we include **fish** in our search for the best biter? In which case, surely **sharks** would have to get a look-in in our jaws hall of fame? But the thing is, no one has ever actually tried **measuring** the bite force of a shark. Well, would **you**? Didn't think so. But scientists can use clever computer models to **predict** the bite forces of certain animals based on information known about their **jaws**, and it turns out that the great white shark could have a bite force of around **4000 psi.**

THAT'S AROUND 15 TIMES STRONGER THAN THE AVERAGE HUMAN BITE, AND MORE THAN TWICE AS STRONG AS THAT OF A JAGUAR OR A HIPPO! BUT REALLY, NO ONE ACTUALLY KNOWS FOR SURE.

But if we're going to judge this bite contest on the most powerful bite ever **tested**, the clear winner would be ... not a mammal ... not a fish ... but a **reptile**. In fact, the **largest** reptile in the world. The **saltwater crocodile.**

HOW DO YOU TEST THE BITE STRENGTH OF A CROCODILE, I HEAR YOU ASK?
VERY CAREFULLY.

Saltwater crocodiles are $\frac{1}{3}$ the length of a **double decker bus** and extremely **strong**, so it takes a team of around **ten croc handlers** to wrestle a "bite force transducer"—which is kinda like a set of waterproof bathroom scales coated in thick leather—into the space between the **croc's back teeth**. Rather them than me. They then get the hungry croc to **bite down** onto a special "metal sandwich" on a pole. Not exactly my idea of a **tasty snack**, but it does the trick. As the croc bites, the transducer wedged between its back teeth **measures the force** of its ferocious snap.

Using this rather **risky-sounding** technique, bite forces of up to 4000 psi have been recorded for the saltwater croc. That's around twice the munch-force of a jaguar or a hippo. A croc's mega bite is thought to be thanks to the **enormous jaw-closing muscles** in its **jowls**—the big fleshy bits hanging down near the back corner of its mouth.

These **mighty muscles** help give the croc its deadly snap, allowing our master crusher to catch and kill animals as big as a **water buffalo**.

But what about if we went **back in time** and looked at all the animals that have ever lived? Who do you think had the bitiest bite **ever?**

WHICH CREATURE HAD THE STRONGEST BITE EVER?

A THE TERRIBLE T. REX

B A COLOSSAL CROCODILE

C A SUPER-SIZED SHARK

D A WHOPPING WHALE

Surely the creature with the strongest bite of all time must have been the mighty **Tyrannosaurus rex**? At an estimated **13,000 psi**, this awesome beast had a biting force **triple** that of the saltwater croc.

But there might have been some **even more** ferocious chompers. Around nine million years ago **giant piranhas** the length of a **baseball bat** swam the rivers of South America.

Scary as they may sound, their **measly** bite force was actually only a couple of times more than that of a modern human. However, they had such **sharp, pointy teeth** that their bite would have been able to cause far more **bone-crushing damage** to your arm than, say, being munched on by your grumpy teenage sister.

While prehistoric piranhas might not have had much going on in the jaw department, the enormous **Deinosuchus**, sometimes known as the **"terrible crocodile,"** was a pretty monstrous muncher. Living around 80 million years ago, it is estimated to have had jaws nearly **twice as strong** as the comparatively puny T. rex.

Topping that, the strongest biter of all time is thought to have been a ginormous shark called **Carcharodon megalodon**. This 65-foot-long mega shark went extinct over 2.6 million years ago, and had an estimated bite force of up to a jaw-dropping 40,000 psi—enough to **crush a small car**. Not a fish I'd like to have met on a prehistoric scuba holiday.

And then there's the **giant prehistoric sperm whale** with a head as long as a racing car and teeth as long as your arm. This **whopping whale** could potentially have topped the bite force of even the mighty megalodon. Unlike modern sperm whales, this colossal creature **had teeth,** suggesting that it probably used its giant jaw for biting.

THE **ANSWER** is **D**
THE CREATURE WITH THE STRONGEST BITE OF ALL TIME WAS PROBABLY A WHOPPING WHALE.

So I'd stay away from **time machines** if I were you. Especially the sort that might eject you into a prehistoric sea.

BUT IF YOU **DO** EVER FIND YOURSELF STUCK IN A TIME WARP AND ABOUT TO BE EATEN FOR LUNCH BY A TERRIBLE CROCODILE, IT MIGHT BE QUITE HELPFUL TO KNOW WHAT TO DO . . .

B PUSH YOUR FINGERS INTO ITS EYES

C COVER ITS NOSTRILS

A PUNCH IT UNDER THE CHIN

WHAT'S THE BEST WAY TO ESCAPE THE GRIP OF A CROCODILE'S JAW?

D STROKE IT TO SLEEP

Given the awesome power of a croc's jaws, the smartest thing would be to **not get caught** by one in the first place. Obviously.

Legend has it that if you **zig-zag** away from an approaching croc at full pelt it won't catch you, but that's a pretty **risky** strategy. And it's also unlikely to work. Even if you run in a straight line. You see, adult crocs can run pretty much **as fast as a human**. So the best thing to do is not to make any sudden movements and to **back away**. Very slowly. While saying your times tables. Actually, don't bother with the times tables—I made that bit up.

IF THE CROC GETS DANGEROUSLY CLOSE TO YOU AND SOMEHOW YOU STILL HAVE YOUR WITS ABOUT YOU, YOU COULD TRY AND HOLD ITS MOUTH SHUT WITH YOUR HANDS.

Amazingly this might actually work. Or at least it might with an **American alligator**. While the jaw muscles of an American alligator are great at **clamping down**, they're **pretty weak** when it comes to **opening** their jaws back up again.

69

BUT IF NONE OF THIS WORKS AND YOU'RE UNLUCKY ENOUGH TO FIND YOURSELF CAUGHT IN A CROC'S TOOTHY GRIP, WHAT NOW?

Well, you could start by trying to **punch** it on the head or under the chin. This worked for a French fisherman who got his head firmly **locked** between the jaws of a saltwater croc in Australia. Thankfully, the croc didn't have a very good grip on him and so, after the brave fisherman delivered a few **punches to the croc's head**, it let him go.

Covering a croc's **nostrils** won't do much good—but a ten-year-old girl did manage to escape from the jaws of an alligator in Florida by **sticking her fingers up its nose**—a trick she'd learned at an alligator park. The startled gator opened its jaws just enough to loosen its grip on her leg. Then she pried its enormous jaws apart and **dashed off**.

If a bit of punching and nostril-poking hasn't scared off your croc, you could try to **hypnotize** it. Seriously. All you have to do is flip it over and **stroke it gently** on its **tummy**.

It's said this ought to be enough to put croccy into a sort of sleep-like **trance**, a form of **natural paralysis**, and its jaws should drop open and release you.

I FOUND IT PRETTY HARD TO BELIEVE THIS CRAZY FACT, SO I DECIDED I WANTED TO TRY IT FOR MYSELF. SO I TOOK A TRIP TO THE AMAZON JUNGLE IN BRAZIL.

71

One night after dark, a small group of us went out onto the river on a little wooden canoe to look for crocodiles. As you do. Suddenly, our local guide, Leo, spotted a **baby croc** in the river. Leo had been flashing his torch around and had caught sight of its eyes **glinting** in the light. Before I'd so much as blinked, crazy Leo nose-dived into the **piranha-infested** water and grabbed the startled little guy . . . and plopped him into my hands.

The baby croc was only just bigger than my palm, and looked like a tiny little **dinosaur**. Leo helped me flip him onto his back and we laid him across my lap. With Leo gently holding him still, I nervously began to **stroke croccy's tummy** with my finger.

Suddenly he stopped wriggling and just **lay there** on his back with his four legs **dangling** out to the sides. He looked like he was fast asleep in bed. Not that baby crocs usually have a bed. Except a **riverbed**. Ha ha.

After a few seconds, we rolled **sleeping croccy** back over . . . and he just jumped back to life. Leo took him from me and gently **plopped** him back into the water, and off he swam.

SO, STROKING A CROC TO SLEEP REALLY DOES WORK. YOU DON'T EVEN HAVE TO SING IT A LULLABY. ALTHOUGH I RECKON TRYING IT OUT ON A FULL-SIZED SNAPPER WOULD PROBABLY PROVE A LITTLE TRICKIER.

73

Some other scary killers can also be **hypnotized out of action** by turning them onto their backs. Sharks, for example. So next time you're face to face with a **great white**, simply flip it over and tickle its tummy and it will fall **fast asleep** for up to 15 minutes. Easy.

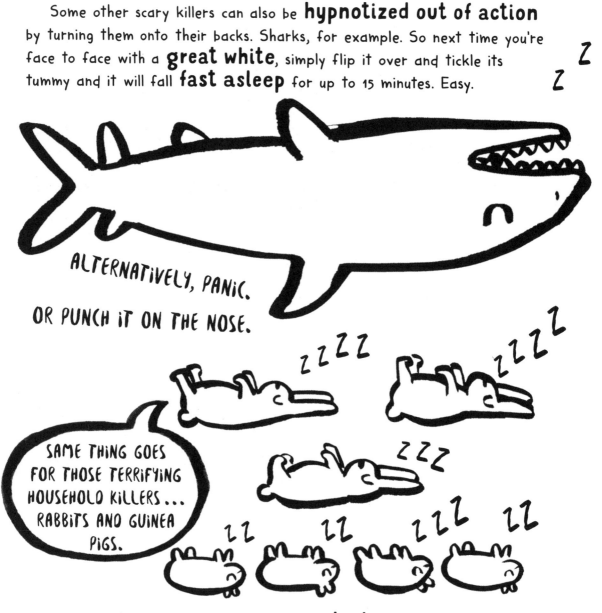

ALTERNATIVELY, PANIC.

OR PUNCH IT ON THE NOSE.

SAME THING GOES FOR THOSE TERRIFYING HOUSEHOLD KILLERS ... RABBITS AND GUINEA PIGS.

Okay, so they're not really that scary, but if you did want to escape from a **killer rabbit attack**, all you'd need to do is **roll** your floppy-eared assailant over a few times and **stroke** her, and she'll probably head straight off to dream land. To wake her, simply **blow on her nose** . . . and she'll suddenly **flip** back over and **hop** into action.

Z

ANYWAY, BACK TO HOW BEST TO ESCAPE FROM A CROC'S JAWS.

Most croc experts agree that the **absolute best** way to deal with a hungry croc is to push your fingers into its eyes. Or you could use a **pencil**. If you happen to have one lying around.

Either way, the startled croc will be so desperate to **protect** the only **sensitive** part of its body that isn't hidden under dense skin or behind a solid mass of bone that it will promptly **relax its jaws** and let go. And you can run off home for milk and cookies. This **finger-pushing** technique did actually save an Australian miner who was attacked by a croc in a creek in Queensland.

THE **ANSWER** is **B** THE **BEST** WAY TO ESCAPE THE GRIP OF A CROCODILE'S JAW IS TO PUSH YOUR FINGERS INTO ITS EYES.

While having your eyes poked out would be pretty **painful** for anyone, it's unlikely that our poor old croc would burst into **tears**. Humans are the only creatures that can produce tears of **sadness**, or any emotion really.

SO CROCODILES CAN'T ACTUALLY CRY WHEN THEY'RE UPSET. NO MATTER HOW MUCH THEY WANT TO.

However, you might have heard someone being accused of **"crying crocodile tears."** This expression is sometimes used to refer to someone who is crying **fake** tears—**pretending** to be sad. Like your sneaky little brother when he's pretending you stole his last **chocolate kiss** so he can get some more.

This strange phrase is thought to have originated from an ancient (but rather silly) belief that crocodiles used to cry in order to **trick their prey** into coming **closer** to them—in order to **gobble** them up. It's possible that this idea came from **real observations** that when crocs are eating they **huff and hiss** and blow out so much air that their eyes might actually **water**, making it **look like** they're having a good old remorseful sob.

SO WHILE A CROCODILE'S TEARS ARE CERTAINLY NOT TEARS OF SADNESS, THEY MAY INDEED EXIST.

DID YOU KNOW THAT BUTTERFLIES HAVE BEEN KNOWN TO DRINK CROCODILE TEARS?

Not so long ago, a butterfly and a bee were spotted sitting on the nose of a **caiman**—a type of small crocodile—in Costa Rica . . . **sipping from its eyes**. For more than 15 minutes the caiman played placidly on a log while the **thirsty** butterfly and bee drank their fill.

You see, while crocodiles might not cry in response to **emotion**, like many other animals they do have **ducts** around their eyes that are similar to human tear ducts. These ducts **produce water** to keep a croc's eyes **moist** and to wash out any **dirt and dust**.

Like human tears, this croc-water also happens to be rich in **salt**, which butterflies are often lacking due to eating only sweet nectar. Sipping on some "crocodile tears" every once in a while is the perfect way for a salt-deprived butterfly to get what he needs. That is, if the croc can **lie still** for long enough. Or he hasn't got a pencil in his eye.

SPEAKING OF PENCILS . . .

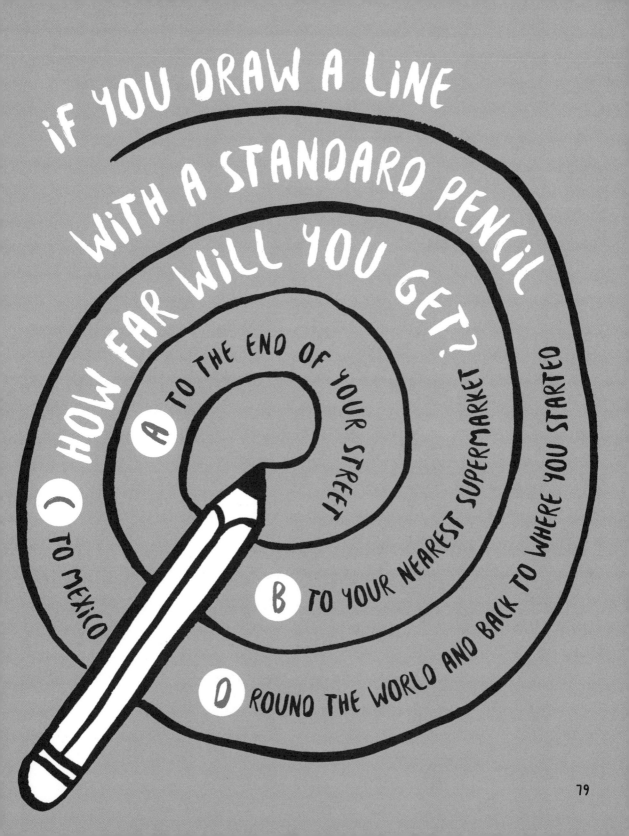

Pencil leads are actually not made of lead at all, they're made of a mixture of **clay** and **graphite**. Graphite is a hard substance made of **carbon**—the same stuff that coal and diamond are made of. In graphite the carbon atoms are arranged in **layers**. These layers are what make graphite so **slippery**. When you slide a pencil across a rough surface, like a piece of paper, **friction** between the paper and the pencil causes some of these super-thin layers of carbon atoms to **slide** over each other and **stick** to the fibers of the paper, leaving behind **silvery lines**.

There are **billions** of carbon atoms in pencil lead, and only a very **small number** of them are left behind on the surface of the paper each time you write something.

In fact, pencil marks are sometimes only a **few ten thousandths** of an inch thick. This means that a pencil can go on writing practically **forever**. Okay, so maybe not forever, but for a pretty long time.

It has been estimated that a pencil can write up to **45,000 words** (that would make for an extremely long history essay) or draw a single line that would stretch for over **35 miles**. We tested this out and we managed to get the pencil to just over 18 miles before it broke. Not bad.

Obviously the distances I suggested in the multiple-choice answers to this question will rather depend on **where you live**. I live only a **short walk** away from my local supermarket, whereas some of you might live in the **countryside** and have to travel by bike or car to pick up your favorite tub of **ice cream**. But I think I can safely assume that **most** of you would find a supermarket within about 20 miles.

THE **ANSWER** is <u>B</u> IF YOU DRAW A LINE WITH A STANDARD PENCIL YOU'D PROBABLY GET TO YOUR NEAREST SUPERMARKET.

IT WOULD BE PRETTY HARD TO FIND A NORMAL PENCIL THAT COULD GET YOU ALL THE WAY TO MEXICO. EVEN IF YOU LIVED IN FLORIDA.

However, the **biggest pencil** in the world is over 65 feet tall, so it's possible that **THAT** could get you to Mexico. But first you'd have to get the **mega pencil** on a plane from the manufacturer's plant in Malaysia. And once you got it home, to get to Mexico you'd probably have to draw lines **under rivers and lakes**. But bizarrely this in itself wouldn't be a problem.

You see, pencils are so smart that they can even write **underwater**. In fact, they can even write in **space!** The sliding off of the graphite layers onto a rough surface is still totally possible under **zero gravity.**

Fountain pens won't write in space, though, as there's no gravity to **pull the ink into the nib**—try writing with one upside down and you'll see what I mean. So pencils had to be used by astronauts until the first **pressurized** "Fisher Space Pen" was produced in 1965. After that, pencils were banned over concerns that the **wood** could easily **catch fire** in a spaceship's pure-oxygen atmosphere.

Despite being super-thin, pencil marks can stay **stuck** to a page for **hundreds of years**. As long as no one **rubs them out**.

Did you know that before **erasers** were invented, people came up with an **unusual** but practical method of getting rid of their mistakes? **Breadcrumbs!** All you needed to do was to **rub** them hard enough on the page to build up some **heat**, and then the breadcrumbs would become **sticky** enough to **lift** the graphite marks off the paper. This is similar to how a modern eraser works.

The most annoying thing about pencils is that they get **shorter**, right? Eventually even your favorite lucky pencil will **shrink** until it's too small to hold and you won't be able to use it.

BUT PENCILS AREN'T THE ONLY THINGS THAT ARE GETTING SHORTER . . .

Wouldn't it be great if there was just a little bit more **time** in the day? Just a few extra minutes to put to good use playing Minecraft or finishing digging that enormous hole in the garden. I mean, it's pretty **awesome** in the autumn when the clocks go back and we gain a **whole extra hour** to lie in bed in the morning. Or carry out secret missions. But sadly, we have to say **goodbye** to that hour again the following spring.

So wouldn't it be fab if **every day** was a bit longer? And we never had to give the extra time back? Well, that's exactly what's happening. Every single day is just **a tiny bit longer** than the day before. Not by much, mind you. I mean, we're talking a really tiny amount of time here.

Like, an increase in day length that amounts to around **two thousandths of a second** over the course of 100 years—not exactly long enough to do anything **useful** with. Like bathe your dog. Or cover your buddy Norman in pudding. But it's definitely **happening**. And the days will keep on getting longer **forever**.

IT FEELS LIKE TIME HAS STOOD STILL FOR ME

85

Well, officially a **day** is the length of time that it takes the Earth to **rotate once** on its axis: to turn all the way around itself, like a slowly rotating spinning top. So if a day is getting **longer**, it follows that the Earth must be turning on its axis **more slowly** each day. Well, it is! And it's all the fault of the **Moon**.

You probably know that **gravity** from the **Earth** pulls on the Moon, keeping it circling above us and stopping it shooting out into space. But did you know that gravity from the Moon **pulls on the surface of the Earth** too? We can't feel this pull as it's far too **weak**, but it affects things that are able to **move freely**. Like **water**. Or possibly **Jell-O**. You won't notice movements in a small bucket of water, or even a large swimming pool. But huge bodies of water like the **oceans** can be very affected by the gravitational pull of the Moon, causing them to **bulge out** toward the Moon in certain places.

These bulges of water are what cause the **tides**. Have you ever been for a **beach walk** at **low tide** and then tried to get back the same way and found the sea has come **swooshing in** and you have to **climb over shells and rocks** to get home? Next time that happens, **blame the Moon.**

Now, the Moon orbits around the Earth **slower** than the Earth turns on its own axis. This means that the Moon is always **lagging slightly behind** the Earth, which makes the Moon **seem** as though it's **moving backward** through the sky. So the Moon's gravity is constantly **pulling backward and upward** on the **oceans**, creating a bulge of "high water." It's almost like the Moon is **scraping** the seawater backward over the surface of the Earth, as the Earth rotates forward underneath it. As the bulge of water drags against the ocean floor, **friction** between the water and the seabed causes the Earth to **slow down** very slightly.

THE EARTH AND THE MOON ARE
SO ENORMOUS THAT IT CAN BE PRETTY HARD TO
REALLY MAKE SENSE OF WHAT'S GOING ON HERE.
SO LET'S TRY A NICE SIMPLE ANALOGY TO
HELP US TO VISUALIZE IT.

Have you ever made a pot? You know, on a wheel? Clay pots are made on one of those spinny things called a **potter's wheel**. The clay rotates like a lump of **sloppy brown goo** on a spinning dinner plate. To make it look pot-like, the potter places her **hands** around the edges of the lump as it spins. In theory, this turns the **potato-shaped lump** into a beautifully shaped pot. Easy. Although in practice it's pretty **tricky** and you can easily end up with **brown slime** all over your face. And the walls.

Anyway, let's imagine that the **spinning pot** represents the **Earth**, and **you,** sitting happily on the stool next to it, are the **Moon.** Now if you stick your **finger** out and place it against the pot as it spins, what happens? The pot keeps spinning but you get a **lump of slimy clay** building up under your finger. This slimy bulge represents what the pull of the Moon does to the **oceans** on the Earth's surface. Except the Moon uses the **invisible force of gravity,** not its finger. Obviously.

Now, if the potter's wheel is spinning freely, the pot will also probably **slow down** a little under your finger. This is because there is **friction** between the layers of clay, so as the outer sloppy layer builds up under your finger it **rubs against** the layers underneath it. The pot has to **work a bit harder** to keep spinning, so it **loses some energy** and **slows down**. Similarly, when the gravity of the Moon **drags** the oceans backward over the Earth's surface, there is **friction** between the water and the sandy seabed. So the Earth **loses some energy** and **slows down a bit** too.

As the pot slows down, some of the **energy** it loses will go into your finger, which will probably get a bit **warm**. Similarly, as the Earth slows down, **the Moon gains energy**. The Moon uses this extra bit of energy to boost itself to a **slightly higher orbit**—an orbit which is a tiny bit **farther** from the Earth and therefore a tiny bit **larger**. This means that the Moon is constantly spiraling very slightly **away from the Earth**. In fact, its **orbit size** increases by about **1 ½ inches a year**—as fast as your **fingernails** grow. That's not really very fast at all.

So the Earth is slowing down, the distance to the Moon is getting greater, and a day is getting longer. But really, not by much. In fact, we gain such a **tiny amount** of time each day that at this rate it'll take around **3.3 million years** for us to get just **1 extra minute**! Not much good if you were hoping for some extra sleep.

Now, seeing as each day is getting longer, you might think that a **year** should be getting longer too. However, a year is defined as the time taken for the Earth to orbit the Sun, which really hasn't changed at all. So a year remains a **constant length.** But to make up for the fact that the days are **longer**, we get slightly **fewer days in each year**. In fact, it's estimated that 350 million years ago there were **385 days** in a year—that's almost 20 more than there are today! But each day was only 23 hours long.

Back to the original question then. If neither a day, nor a year, nor the distance to the Moon are getting shorter, then what is? That only leaves poor old **Mount Etna.**

COULD SHE REALLY BE GETTING SHORTER?

Mount Etna is Europe's most active **volcano** and is found on an island called **Sicily**, off the south coast of Italy. Believe it or not, scientists have recently discovered that the whole volcano is **moving**! It is **sliding downward toward the sea.** Almost as if it's trying to go for a quick dip to cool down. Etna's not exactly moving **fast**—at only **half an inch a year** even a **snail** could move faster. And a very lazy snail at that. Etna is probably sliding because it's sitting on a bed of **soft rock**, just like the **Leaning Tower of Pisa**.

Anyway, Etna's **descent** is really nothing to worry about, but it's pretty exciting as it's the first time that an **entire active volcano** has been seen to move!

By the way, it's not only the Moon that can influence the Earth's spin. Changes in **sea levels** can also have an effect, like those that happened after **ice ages** or are happening right now due to **global warming**. And so can **earthquakes**. In 2011 an earthquake in Japan moved sections of the Earth's crust slightly **inward**, toward the center of the Earth. This made the Earth **speed up** a tiny bit, kind of like how if an ice skater brings his **arms in**

THE **ANSWER** is **D**
MOUNT ETNA APPEARS TO BE GETTING SHORTER AS IT IS SLIDING DOWNHILL TOWARD THE SEA.

toward his body during a spin he'll rotate **faster**. This giant quake **shortened the length of a day** by 1.8 millionths of a second. Not quite enough to counteract the day-lengthening effect of the Moon, but enough to be detected by an atomic clock.

SO DO YOU RECKON IF YOU GOT ENOUGH OF YOUR FRIENDS TO JUMP UP AND DOWN AT THE SAME TIME AS YOU, YOU COULD CAUSE AN EARTHQUAKE BIG ENOUGH TO MAKE THE EARTH TURN FASTER?

In February 2016, a group of **geology** students from the University of Leicester decided to install some **earthquake-detecting** equipment in a local primary school. It was designed to work alongside apparatus in their university laboratories to help them take measurements of the **vibrations** of the Earth. A few days later they were surprised to notice an unexpected peak in **ground wobbles**—what's known as **seismic activity**. The students weren't quite sure **why** this was, but they assumed it was just a small natural **earth tremor**.

But then one of the geologists noticed something weird. The tremor had occurred at around the **same time** that a **soccer match** had been taking place at a stadium roughly half a mile away from the school. When she took a closer look, she realized that the earth tremor had occurred at the **exact same moment** that striker Leonardo Ulloa had scored a **gasp-inducing** winning goal for Leicester City—in the very last minute of the match. Ulloa's goal had caused such **excitement** in the home crowd that they had all **simultaneously leaped into the air**, roaring with joy. As they landed on the ground, the Earth literally **shook**.

The resulting **vibrations** measured 0.3 on the **Richter scale**—a scale used to indicate exactly how much the Earth shakes during an earthquake.

Now, a value of 0.3 is far too small for anyone to actually **feel** any ground wobbling, let alone for it to be classified as an actual earthquake. But it's definitely **something**.

The following year a similar thing happened in Spain—and this time it was at a much **larger stadium**. Barcelona was playing Paris Saint-Germain (also known as PSG) in the Champions League and the match was taking place at the enormous Camp Nou stadium, home to the Barcelona team. Camp Nou holds nearly **100,000 people**—more than three times as many people as the stadium in Leicester.

It was a super-tense match. Barcelona was already losing 0-4 to PSG from the first leg of the competition. To the home crowd's excitement, Barcelona scored a stunning **three goals** in the first hour, taking things to 3-4. The atmosphere in the stadium was **electric**.

Could they equalize? But then **disaster struck** as PSG scored again. Gah! The score was 3-5. Surely it was all over? But then something **incredible** happened. In the 88th minute Barcelona scored another goal. Then, three minutes later, another. And then, three minutes later, **another!** Now the crowd was on the **edge** of their seats.

While a value of 1.0 still isn't quite enough for anyone to have actually been able to **feel** that Roberto made the Earth move, it definitely qualified as a **"microearthquake."**

GOAL!

So when Barcelona's Sergi Roberto scored a **final goal** in the **95th minute**, the crowd went absolutely **wild**. As they all **leaped to their feet** in utter disbelief at one of the greatest **comebacks** in the history of soccer, scientists at an Institute of Earth Sciences half a mile away recorded **ground movements** that measured **1.0** on the Richter Scale.

THE **ANSWER** is (100,000 PEOPLE JUMPING IN THE AIR AT THE SAME TIME CAN MAKE THE GROUND MOVE AS MUCH AS AN EARTHQUAKE.

Microearthquakes measuring 1.0 on the Richter scale aren't really that big a deal. In fact, they occur over a million times a year. For an earthquake to really **feel** like an earthquake, it needs to measure at least 3.0. Then you'd get a bit of **ground shaking** and maybe some **rattling** of your mom's ornaments on the living room shelves . . . and a rather scared puppy.

COULD WE ACHIEVE A QUAKE THIS HIGH ON THE RICHTER SCALE JUST BY JUMPING?

The Richter Scale is a funny old scale. For a value on the scale to go up by a single point, the strength of a ground tremor would have to increase by a **factor of ten.** It's what's called a **logarithmic scale.** This means that in order for us to go from a goal-scoring 1.0 to an ornament-rattling 3.0, the ground would have to shake **100 times more violently** than during the Barcelona football match. That would probably require around **10 million people** all jumping at once!

In the UK there are around **65 million people**. So if somehow you managed to get everyone in the UK to jump in the air at **exactly the same time** (I've no idea how, but I'd like to see you try), we'd be sure to feel **something.** Well, actually we wouldn't, as we'd be the ones doing the jumping, but you know what I mean.

Most major earthquakes measure more than **6.0** on the Richter scale. That's a whopping **1,000 times more intense** than a 3.0 quake. These scary earthquakes result in **violent** earth shaking and can do major **damage** to buildings. By my calculations, **10 billion people** jumping at once could **in theory** cause a quake like this—but that's more than the population of the **entire planet**! What about if all the **animals** on the planet jumped too? Now this is just getting silly. But seriously, there's an awful lot of **sheep** on the planet. What if they jumped with us? What if they sweated a lot? Then maybe we'd get **sweaters!** Ha ha. Okay, sorry. I'll stop now.

OFTEN IT'S NOT THE SHAKY EARTH ITSELF THAT CAUSES THE MOST DAMAGE DURING AN EARTHQUAKE. IT'S BUILDINGS COLLAPSING. AN ARCHITECT IN JAPAN HAS COME UP WITH A RATHER UNEXPECTED SOLUTION FOR THIS . . .

Have you ever noticed that the buildings that **topple over** in an earthquake are not always the ones you'd expect? For example, sometimes a quake will cause lots of **medium-sized** buildings to crumble to the ground, while the short ones and the skyscrapers are left standing strong. It's a bit **weird** isn't it?

You see, what determines whether a building will collapse in a quake is partly what it's **made of,** but is also due to the building's **resonant frequency**. This is the number of times each second that a building **likes to wobble at**.

FREQUENCY = NUMBER OF TIMES SOMETHING HAPPENS PER SECOND.

Pretty much **everything** has a resonant frequency that, given half the chance, it likes to shake at. Including your **kitchen.** Like a salt shaker. This is why if you push your little sister on a **swing** she'll keep on swinging backward and forward **the same number of times each second**—no matter how hard you push her. Try it next time you're in the park. Give her a push, then time how long it takes for her to **swing back** to you. It should always be the **same amount of time** between each swing. That's the time that **particular** swing **prefers** to swing for. And it's pretty hard to make it swing any other way.

Now, **tall** or **long** things prefer to take **longer** to wobble or swing than short or small things, so they complete fewer swings each second. They are said to have a **lower resonant frequency**. Ever noticed how the long arm in a **grandfather clock** takes longer to swing backward and forward than the short arm in a **cuckoo clock**?

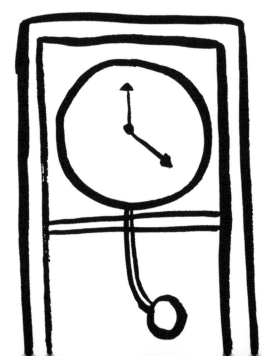

RESONANT FREQUENCY = NUMBER OF TIMES SOMETHING NATURALLY VIBRATES OR SWINGS PER SECOND.

Okay, so imagine there's a big table and on it are **three plates of Jell-O**. One is an enormously tall Jell-O, perhaps as big as a **boot**. Another is a medium sized Jell-O, the size of your **face**. And the third is a wee little Jell-O, only as big as a **marshmallow**. Give the table a little **jiggle** and you'll probably notice that the tall Jell-O starts to **sway slowly back and forth**, the middle one does rather a **dignified wobble**, while the little one does a frenetic little **booty-shaking jiggle**. Just like swings, the shorter the Jell-O, the higher its resonant frequency and the more **frantic** its natural wobble is.

Next time you're eating Jell-O, wait before you take a mouthful and see how fast it wobbles on the spoon.

Now, if you carefully pick up the big Jell-O plate and slowly move it backward and forward, you'll find a **pace** at which your movements **match** the **preferred sway frequency** of the Jell-O. The big Jell-O will start to sway **much more** than it did before. The Jell-O is picking up **energy** from your frequency-matched plate movements and is **really** starting to move now. This is called **resonance.**

Resonance explains what happened when people started accidentally walking over the Millennium Bridge in London **at the same pace** that the bridge naturally preferred to wobble at. It suddenly started **swinging wildly** from side to side and had to be closed. It was picking up energy and **resonating.**

So what's all this got to do with **earthquakes?** Well, earthquakes cause the ground to **shake and wobble** back and forth, just like when you were wobbling the Jell-O plates. The frequency of the ground-wobbles, or **vibrations**, depends on what **type of rock** it is made from. **Hard bedrock** likes to vibrate at high frequencies, while **soft sediments** naturally vibrate at much lower frequencies. And, just like Jell-O, **tall buildings** like to wobble at a lower frequency than **short buildings**. So if an earthquake shakes the ground at the **same frequency** as the building built above it *likes* to wobble at...

THE BUILDING GETS A WHOLE LOAD OF ENERGY AND DOES A LOT OF CRAZY WOBBLING, UNTIL SOMETIMES THE WALLS BREAK AND CRUMBLE TO THE FLOOR.

BOOM!

So, quakes on rocks that like to wobble at **medium** frequencies will only cause **medium-height** buildings to collapse—the small ones and skyscrapers will be just **fine!**

So one way to help protect a building from an earthquake is to try to make sure that the building's **natural wobble-frequency** (its resonant frequency) is **not** the same as the resonant frequency of the **rocks** it's built on.

The **other** important factor is what the building is **made of**. Now you'd think that something **strong** like concrete would be best for buildings. But actually this isn't always the case. Concrete might be strong but it is also really **heavy**, and this isn't great when it comes to wobbling. You see, heavy things have lots of **inertia**—they don't like **getting going**, but once they're moving it's pretty hard to **stop** them. Like a rhino on a skateboard.

This means that once heavy concrete buildings **start** wobbling, they'll **really** wobble and it'll be pretty hard to stop them. And, not only that, but if they do **crash down** they'll cause an awful lot of **damage**.

WHEEEE!

I WOULDN'T WANT TO GET IN THE WAY OF THAT SKATEBOARDING RHINO, WOULD YOU?

It turns out that the **best** types of materials when it comes to safer wobbling are slightly **flexible** materials. Like **wood**. Wood may not **seem** particularly flexible, but you can really tell the difference if you throw a brick and a log at a wall. Which one will do the most damage? You might also have noticed that you can **bounce** on a tree branch.

Wooden floorboards can **stretch** and **creak**—and so can wooden walls. This means that wooden buildings can withstand a lot more shaking and wobbling **before they collapse** than concrete buildings can. And if they **do** collapse, wooden walls will **absorb** more of the **energy of the quake**—and so will do far less damage as they fall.

WOULD YOU RATHER A BRICK OR A LOG FELL ON YOUR HEAD? IDEALLY NEITHER, OBVIOUSLY.

BUT CAN WE GO ONE STEP BETTER THAN WOOD?

In 2013 a Japanese architect was asked to come up with a design for an **earthquake-resistant church**. Naturally, he decided to make it out of . . . **cardboard**. You see, this architect was well known across the world for designing cardboard buildings. The design he came up with used **98 giant cardboard tubes** coated with a waterproof substance called **polyurethane**, with wooden beams for reinforcement—all under a waterproof roof. This cardboard church was erected in Christchurch, New Zealand, and its walls are so **light** and **flexible**, they're much safer than concrete should an earthquake strike.

Not only is the flexible cardboard far **less likely to snap** and collapse, but even if it did it would do less damage to the people inside than having concrete come crashing down around them. This **crazy creation** is even fireproof, rainproof, and big enough to hold 700 people . . . and is predicted to last at least **50 years!**

THE **ANSWER** is **B**
CARDBOARD HAS BEEN USED TO BUILD AN EARTHQUAKE-PROOF BUILDING.

SO IT TURNS OUT THAT CARDBOARD MIGHT BE STRONGER THAN YOU THINK. BUT COULD **THINKING** ACTUALLY **MAKE YOU** STRONGER?

WHAT MIGHT MAKE YOUR MUSCLES STRONGER?

A THINKING ABOUT THEM

B PAINTING THEM RED

C PUTTING THEM IN A BUCKET OF COLD WATER

D WEARING A SUPERMAN T-SHIRT

Not so long ago, some scientists persuaded a group of volunteers to each put their arm in a **plaster cast** for a month. The awkward cast meant that the volunteers couldn't move their wrists—pretty annoying if they'd wanted to play the violin.

Half the volunteers were asked to spend a solid 11 minutes of each day just **thinking about** moving their hand up and down.

Another group of volunteers were given the **same** plaster cast but were told **not to** think about waggling their wrists.

Perhaps they thought about peanut butter instead. Or unicorns. This is what in science we call **a fair test.** (Not the unicorn bit.)

At the end of the month the casts were removed and the strength of all the volunteers' wrist muscles were tested. And would you **believe it?** The muscles of the group who had thought about wrist-waggling were **twice as strong** as those who'd thought about something rather less ... er ... odd.

THE **ANSWER** is **A**
THINKING ABOUT YOUR MUSCLES MIGHT MAKE THEM STRONGER.

Does this mean we can get **muscly thighs** by sitting playing computer games all weekend while **thinking about** running after evil aliens, rather than getting off our **butts** and actually going to sports practice? Well, imaginary exercise certainly seems to activate the **same part of the brain** as real exercise. However it's unlikely that it can actually make our muscles get any **bigger.**

So how does it work? The thing is, we don't always use all the available **parts** of our muscles. For example, some parts of our calf muscles just sit there lazily doing nothing while we try and force the other parts to get to 100 bounces on a trampoline. This means we have the **potential** to be stronger than we are, simply by using more of the muscle that's already there. So **thinking** about exercising our muscles is a bit like **practicing** the skill of using them. So then the next time we hop on a trampoline we are able to use a **bigger section** of our existing leg muscles to help us bounce higher. Sneaky! This **mental practice** technique is a trick often used by top athletes.

WHAT ABOUT THE COLD WATER iDEA?

Was this a sensible suggestion? In a word, no. If you want to strengthen your muscles, the **last** thing you should do is to put them in a bucket of cold water. If your muscles get cold they'll actually probably get **weaker**, as in cold conditions it's harder for muscles to get the **oxygen** they need in order to contract. The chances are that immersing your arms in a bucket of cold water will make them **weaker** rather than stronger.

Bizarrely, there might actually be a grain of truth in the idea that **wearing a Superman T-shirt** can make you stronger. Just a very small grain, mind you. In a recent experiment, Superman-clothed university students seemed to **feel** that they were stronger. When they were given weights to lift, of course they couldn't **actually** lift anything heavier than usual—but they certainly **thought** they could! It seems that the T-shirts made them **feel super strong.**

SUPERMAN MIGHT BE STRONG, BUT EVEN OUR MUSCLY SUPERHERO WOULD WORK UP **QUITE A SWEAT** IF HE HAD TO LIFT SOMETHING RATHER BIG AND HEAVY. LIKE A **RHINOCEROS** PERHAPS.

Or **would** he? Did you know that some people don't actually sweat?

SERIOUSLY, NOT A WHIFF!

You might be surprised to hear that the average adult **sweats** around **two cups** a day. That's enough juicy sweat to fill a small water bottle. Ewwww. In fact, if your big sister went for a run on a hot day, she could probably produce up to **four cups** of the stuff **every hour!** That's a whole lot of sweat. Imagine giving her a good ole' sniff under the armpits when she comes home for dinner. No thanks!

But actually **fresh** sweat doesn't smell. In fact you could wipe the sweat from her **two to five million** sweat glands all over your face quite happily. Or even someone else's face. But please ask them first.

YOU SEE, IT'S NOT THE SWEAT ITSELF BUT THE BACTERIA THAT LIVE ON OUR SKIN THAT CAN CAUSE US TO GET A BIT STINKY. THESE BACTERIA **FEED** ON SWEAT, SLOWLY BREAKING IT DOWN INTO SMELLY CHEMICALS THAT CAN BE DETECTED BY OUR NOSES. AND OTHER PEOPLE'S NOSES.

Interestingly, the bacteria that are the most revolting stink-producers grow best on **artificial polyester** clothes, but not so well on **natural fibers** like cotton. So if you want to avoid being a little pungent after soccer practice, stick to cotton T-shirts—and chuck them in the washing machine (and chuck yourself in the shower) soon after exercising. Some people also like to wear a **deodorant** to neutralize the smell, and an **antiperspirant** to reduce the amount of sweat they produce in the first place.

But what most people don't know is that not everyone actually sweats the **same amount**. In fact, there's a whole load of **odor-free** people out there who hardly sweat at all—and who might have been wearing deodorant for years for **no reason**.

The amount we sweat is controlled, at least in part, by a particular **gene**.

A gene is a set of **instructions** that is found in the cells of our body, and it tells the body what to do. This particular gene doesn't just affect how much sweat ends up on our **skin**, but also how much sweat ends up in all sorts of other places. Including **inside our ears**. Here, our sweat combines with **dead skin cells** and other chemicals, forming . . . wait for it . . .

EARWAX

Now, most people from Europe and Africa have a version of this sweating gene that makes them produce **lots** of sweat, so they end up with **sweaty skin** and **sticky golden-brown earwax**. Which is handy, as it sticks nicely to wherever you decide to hide it after a good ear-pick.

But about 2 percent of people from Europe and Africa have a **different** version of the gene, meaning they produce less sweat and their earwax ends up **gray** and **dry** and **flaky**. Interestingly, while this low-sweating, dry-earwaxy version of the gene is quite rare in Europeans and Africans, it is far more common in people from **East Asia**.

THE **ANSWER** is **A**
THE TYPE OF EARWAX YOU HAVE MIGHT INDICATE HOW MUCH YOU SWEAT.

Studies suggest that many dry-earwaxy-type people have **no idea** that they don't sweat very much, as they've been wearing deodorant for so long. They probably just think their deodorant works rather well. They may, however, have noticed their **flaky** earwax.

So before your big sister buys her next expensive deodorant, tell her she should probably check her earwax type. She might think you're a bit **nutty**, but tell her if it's dry and flaky she needn't bother with the deodorant, as she probably doesn't sweat enough to need it. And then give her a big **armpitty** hug.

YOU MIGHT BE INTERESTED TO KNOW THAT THERE'S AN ANIMAL THAT FINDS A RATHER INTERESTING USE FOR ITS SWEAT . . .

Sweating is one of the best ways to keep **cool.** Well, aside from taking off all your clothes, that is. Which is probably not a good idea if you're at a party.

Your body is covered in millions of tiny **sweat glands**. When you get hot, these glands secrete small amounts of **salty fluid** onto the surface of your skin—especially under your arms, and places like your feet and forehead. The water in the sweaty fluid then **evaporates**, using some of the **heat energy** in your skin to turn it into vapor.

SO AS THE WATER TURNS TO VAPOR YOUR SKIN LOSES HEAT AND YOUR BODY COOLS DOWN.

That's why if you've been playing an intense game of football and you **wipe your sweaty face** with a towel—or more likely your sleeve—you won't actually cool down very much. You might make yourself **look** slightly more appropriate for family dinner, but if you get rid of the sweat **before it has time to evaporate** it won't do nearly as good a job at cooling you down. Tell that to your mom the next time you come to the **dinner table** a sweaty mess.

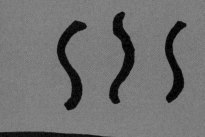

We can also lose heat **directly** through our skin. When we get warm, in a valiant effort to cool us down, the **vessels carrying blood** close to the **surface** of our skin get a bit **wider.** This means that more of our nice warm blood flows close to the surface of our body. We can then lose some of this heat straight off our skin by a process called **radiation**, cooling us down. If you know someone with quite pale skin you might even be able to **see** this happening. When they get hot their skin might get a bit **redder**, as their **warm red blood** moves close to the surface. If you **stand close** to them you may even **feel** some heat radiating off them.

Most **animals** lose heat in much the same way as us, through sweating and by radiation from their skin. But the trouble is, big **bulky** animals have a rather small amount of **body surface** (through which they can lose heat), compared to the **enormous volume** of their body. So they have a pretty hard time cooling themselves down.

That's why big animals that live in really hot areas, like camels, tend to be really **skinny**. That way they have lots of skin to cool down through and not so much **stuff inside them** to get hot in the first place.

BUT WHAT ABOUT A BIG FAT ELEPHANT?

Elephants are the largest living land animals, and they're not exactly skinny minnies. Plus, their skin is **super-thick** and **tough**—so they can push their way through spiny bushes and trees—which means they **can't lose much heat** through their skin.

So elephants really **struggle** to keep themselves **cool**. This problem is made far worse by the fact that **elephants can't sweat!** Their thick skin doesn't contain any sweat glands. So how on earth do these **sweatless hulks** keep cool?

WELL, SCATTERED OVER THEIR ENORMOUS BODIES ARE A DOZEN OR SO SMALL "THERMAL WINDOWS"— LITTLE PATCHES WHERE THEIR SKIN IS A LOT THINNER AND WHERE THERE ARE LOTS OF BLOOD VESSELS RUNNING CLOSE TO THE SURFACE.

They also have thin skin on the **inside of their ears**. So elephants cool down by losing lots of heat energy directly from their skin in these specific areas. Plus you've probably seen them **flapping** their enormous ears around like a fan to create a nice breeze. And they're often found **splashing about** in rivers and **spraying** themselves with cooling water.

133

Hang on. Confession time. When I said that elephants can't sweat, that wasn't **entirely** true. **Sorry.** Bizarrely, they do have just a few sweat glands . . . **between their toes!** Not that they do much good there. Our sweaty-toed, trunk-wielding friends are not the only animals to have sweat glands confined to their pinkies.

> DOGS, LiKE MOST OF OUR FURRY FRiENDS, CAN ONLY SWEAT THROUGH THE PARTS OF THEiR BODY THAT ARE NOT COVERED iN FUR, WHiCH BASiCALLY ONLY LEAVES THEiR NOSE AND THEiR TOES—WELL, PAW PADS.

> A DOG'S THiCK FUR ALSO PROTECTS THE DOG FROM THE HARMFUL ULTRAViOLET RAYS OF THE SUN.

Paw-sweating isn't exactly a very **efficient** way of losing heat, but you probably know what a **hot dog** does instead . . . covers itself in mustard. No, sorry, that's a bad joke. A hot dog sticks out its tongue and **pants**. Saliva **evaporates** off the dog's long wet tongue, carrying away some of the heat energy as it turns to vapor—just like our sweat does on our skin.

This brings us neatly on to hippos. **Hippos** are one of the few land animals that aren't covered in fur. Well, would **you** wear a fur coat if you spent half your day **lolling around** in very **muddy** water? Your coat would get horribly **matted** and **waterlogged** and might never dry off!

So it's rather **sensible** that hippos have evolved not to have fur. However, this means that poor old hippos are terribly sensitive to getting **sunburned**. This is a big problem, especially as they usually live in very **hot sunny** places.

To get around this problem, evolution has equipped hippos with a very clever way of **protecting** themselves from the damaging effects of the sun's rays. They sweat. **A lot**. And it's red. **Red?** Well, kind of orangey-red. So much so that the ancient Greeks used to think that hippos sweated **blood.**

Strictly speaking, this red stuff is not actually sweat; it's an oily substance consisting of two chemicals, aptly named **hipposudoric acid** and **norhipposudoric acid**. When these acids are released they're **transparent**, but when they get exposed to the sun the first one quickly turns **red** and the second one turns **orange** . . . and together they act as a **sunblock!** The red one also works as an **antiseptic**, preventing the grumpy hippo's many cuts and scratches—mostly from fighting other hippos—from getting **infected**.

THE ANSWER is C
A HIPPO USES iTS SWEAT AS A SUNSCREEN.

It's not just a hippo's sweat that's **strangely colored**. So is its **milk**. The red and orange acids combine with the white milk . . . so the milk comes out **pink!** Did you know that a cup of pink hippo milk contains more **calories** than a **cheeseburger?** Like all mammals, hippos use this super-nutritious milk to feed their babies . . . who are sometimes born **underwater**. Talk about a water baby. Awww.

Hippos are not the only fur-free animals that have come up with a **clever** way to **protect** themselves from the sun. You see, it's not only **land** animals that need protection—even creatures living in the **deep blue sea** are exposed to the sun's harmful rays!

HANG ON A SEC . . . BEFORE WE TALK ABOUT SUNBURNED FISH, HAVE YOU EVER WONDERED WHY THE SEA IS BLUE?

WHY IS THE SEA BLUE?

C THERE ARE BLUE PLANKTON IN THE SEA

B IT ABSORBS LESS BLUE LIGHT

A IT IS HOME TO LOTS OF BLUE WHALES

D THE SEA REFLECTS THE SKY

Have you ever seen those holiday-brochure photos of people in **warm** locations, sunning themselves on sandy white beaches surrounded by crystal clear blue sea? You might be thinking "Why them? Why not me? It's not **fair!** Why do I have to go to school?!" But have you ever thought, "Why **blue?!**" Okay, probably not. But let's face it, blue is a bit of a random color isn't it? Seems a bit, well, **chilly** to me.

139

Well, the reason the sea looks blue is to do with the light from the sun that falls on it. Sunlight exists as what's called a **spectrum** of light waves. It forms part of the **electromagnetic spectrum**, which includes many types of waves of different **wavelengths**, with radio waves and microwaves at one end and X-rays and gamma rays at the other. Sunlight consists mainly of the bit in the middle of the spectrum, called **visible light.**

So even though sunlight usually looks yellowy-white, it's actually a **mixture** of lots of different colors. We can see this demonstrated when sunlight shines through **raindrops** on a sunny day . . . and the white light splits into a beautiful **rainbow.**

I'd heard that rainbows often form near powerful **waterfalls** in **hot countries**, where there are lots of **water droplets** in the air and it's very **sunny**. So I thought I'd check it out. I went to visit the incredible **Iguazu Falls**, which are a series of spectacular waterfalls on the border between Brazil and Argentina—together making up the largest waterfall system in the world. And to my delight I saw countless **beautiful rainbows**. Even some **double** and **triple** ones!

Anyway, back to the point. If we go **beyond** the red end of the spectrum of visible light, toward the radio-waves end of the electromagnetic spectrum, we get to what's called **infrared light.**

We can't really see this type of light but we can **feel** it as heat—this is why we feel heat from the sun and why hot things **glow red.** Like a toaster.

Infrared rays can be detected by special cameras which allow us to "see" warm things in the dark: useful if you want to **spy** on your dog at night.

SOLDIERS USE INFRARED GLASSES TO HELP THEM FIND THEIR WAY AT NIGHT.

At the other end of the visible spectrum—beyond the blue end—is **ultraviolet light**, or UV. UV rays cause **sunburn** and can do damage to our bodies. Which isn't very cool. But they can also be used for sending **secret messages!** Certain substances don't show up under normal light but **glow** when UV light is shone on them, so they can be used to make **invisible ink**. Invisible paints can also make fun Halloween costumes—assuming your host has a UV lamp.

marks the spot

If you don't have any invisible paint you could always use . . . **dog pee**. Dog urine glows under UV light due to all the **protein** in the meaty food that dogs eat.

I'm not seriously suggesting you cover your best party outfit in dog pee. Please don't. But it could work as invisible ink in an **emergency**.

So what's all this got to do with the color of the sea? Well, sunlight is **absorbed** by water, so some of it kinda **disappears** as it travels through the sea. That's why the deeper underwater you go, the **darker** it gets. But the weird thing is, different parts of the spectrum of light get absorbed by **different amounts.** Light at the **red** and **infrared** end of the spectrum gets absorbed the **most.**

This leaves behind more of the **blue** and **ultraviolet** light rays to either travel down **deeper** into the water or to get **scattered** by the water. Which means that lots of the blue light can end up bouncing back out of the water . . . and straight into your eyes. **So this is why the sea looks blue!!** And it's also why the deeper you go, the **deeper blue** it looks.

Particles such as **sand** and **silt** also affect the exact color of seawater. And in some areas, the presence of lots of tiny **slimy green algae**, called phytoplankton, can turn the ocean a beautiful turquoise-blue. So next time you envy the people on the **paradise beach holiday,** remember they're swimming through slime.

THE ANSWER is B

THE SEA LOOKS BLUE BECAUSE iT ABSORBS LESS BLUE LiGHT THAN RED LiGHT.

The fact that blue light can travel quite deep into the ocean means that even if you're several feet **underwater** you might still be **exposed** to the harmful UV rays of the sun. In fact, as long as you can still **see** light, there's probably a bit of UV there. This means that you can get **sunburned** even when you're **swimming underwater!** And so can a fish.

The small stripy **zebrafish** has come up with a nifty solution for this. It produces a substance called **gadusol** that acts as a sort of **sunscreen**. Kinda like the hippo's **pink sweat** that we talked about in the last question. It's thought that similar chemicals to gadusol might also be found in other types of fish and sea urchins, and even in some birds and reptiles. Scientists hope that one day it might be possible to make a **pill** containing this clever **fishy chemical** and give it to humans to eat . . . so we can produce our own sunscreen! How **cool** is that?! So perhaps in the future we won't have to **slather** white stuff all over ourselves before we go to the beach.

But until then, please use sunscreen. Especially when you're **swimming** outdoors. Lots of people don't realize that you can actually get **more** sunburned swimming than you can just sitting on the beach building sandcastles. Or burying your dog. This is because if some of your skin is **just above the surface** of the water, not only are there some UV rays from the sun hitting you **directly** from above, but

some of the UV rays that **miss** your body and enter the water around you are **scattered** back out of the water . . . and onto your body. **Double whammy!** So watch your back when you're snorkeling. And not just because your annoying brother might water-bomb you.

SO PRODUCING OUR OWN SUNSCREEN, LIKE OUR HiPPO ANO FiSHY FRIENDS, WOULD OEFINITELY BE PRETTY USEFUL. ESPECIALLY iF WE LIVED SOMEWHERE WHERE THE SUNNY OAYS WERE REALLY LONG . . .

THIS STRANGE—
SOUNDING FACT IS ALL
ABOUT HOW WE DEFINE
A DAY AND A YEAR.

A year is defined as the time it takes for a planet to travel all the way around the sun. This is called its **orbit**. For the Earth, this journey takes **365¼ days**.

Hang on, you might be thinking. "You can't have a quarter of a day in a year!" **Quite right**. So every four years we add up these extra quarters, and that year has a whole extra day—on **February 29th**. We call this a **leap year**.

SO HOW DO WE DEFINE A DAY?

A day is the time that it takes a planet to rotate once on its **axis**: to turn all the way around itself, like a slowly rotating **spinning top**. If you are standing on a part of the Earth that is **facing the sun**, it is daytime. As the Earth turns on its axis, halfway around you will find yourself **facing away from the sun** in complete darkness. It is now nighttime. You won't be able to see a thing, not even the end of your nose—unless of course you turn the lights on. Obviously. Although to be fair, you can't actually **see** the end of your nose anyway. Unless you go **cross-eyed**. Or **can you?** Actually, you can **always** see your nose but your brain just **filters** it out! How cool is that?!

ANYWAY, SORRY, WHERE WAS I?

Ah yes, **nighttime**. Luckily the Earth keeps on turning all the way through the night until you end up in pretty much the same place you started: facing the sun again, in broad **daylight**. It takes almost exactly **24 hours** for the Earth to do this complete day–night cycle, from one **sunrise** to the next.

So, how do these day and year definitions help us to understand this **strange idea** that there could be a planet on which a day lasts longer than a year? Maybe you guessed that the answer has something to do with how **far** the planets are from the sun. Well, you'd be right. Partly.

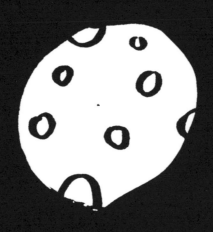

Let's take a look at **Venus**. Now, Venus is **closer** to the sun than the Earth is, so not only is its orbit around the sun **smaller** than ours, but it also travels **faster** than us, as the force of gravity pulling it toward the sun is greater—so it has to travel faster to maintain its orbit. Therefore it takes Venus **less time** than Earth to make a complete circuit around the sun. This means a year on Venus is **shorter** than a year on Earth. In fact it is only around 224 Earth-days. Makes sense so far. **Phew.**

But what's really strange about Venus is that it turns on its axis really really **slowly**. Soooo slowly that it takes Venus a whopping **243 Earth-days** to rotate just **once**. Which means that by the time Venus has completed its 224–Earth-day year, it won't have even finished turning **once** on its axis. So a **day** on Venus lasts even longer than a **year** on Venus. If you lived there you'd have your birthday **every day**. Sometimes twice!

THE **ANSWER** is **B**
ON VENUS A DAY LASTS
LONGER THAN A YEAR.

But the real question is **why** does Venus turn so **slowly?** Scientists don't really know for sure, but one **theory** is that a long long time ago Venus was merrily spinning around when it underwent a **huge collision** with another object in space, like a **big rock** or something. This mighty **crash** could have caused Venus's spinning to **slow right down.** It's thought that the collision might even have flipped Venus **upside down**, which would neatly explain why Venus spins **backward** compared to most of the other planets—this is what we call **retrograde motion.** So on Venus, the sun rises in the west . . . and sets in the east!

BOiiNGG!

IF YOU THINK VENUS'S MEGA-LONG DAY IS WEIRD, THERE IS ANOTHER PLANET ON WHICH IT CAN STAY DARK FOR NEARLY 21 YEARS AT A TIME . . .

ON WHiCH PLANET MiGHT iT STAY DARK FOR 21 YEARS AT A TiME?

 JUPiTER

 SATURN

 URANUS

 NEPTUNE

To make sense of this **strange** fact it would help to understand a bit about the **seasons**.

If you live on Earth (which I assume you do if you're reading this book) and you live a reasonable distance from the **equator**, you'll experience seasons. This is because the Earth doesn't spin bolt upright; it is slightly **tilted**, by about 23.5 degrees. So as the Earth travels on its merry way around the sun, when the part of the Earth you're living on is tilted **toward** the sun you will get **more direct sunlight** than you would for the rest of the year, and you will experience **more hours of daylight** than usual. So the days will be **warmer** and it will stay **light** for longer. This will occur for about a quarter of the Earth's orbit. We call this period of time **summer**. If you're living north of the equator, in what we call the **Northern Hemisphere**, this happens between June and August. At the **peak** of summer, the North Pole will be in **constant daylight**.

DID YOU KNOW THAT IN THE SOUTHERN HEMISPHERE IT IS SUMMER AT CHRISTMAS?

And this works the other way around too. For a quarter of the Earth's orbit, your part of the Earth will be tilted **away** from the sun, so the sun's rays will not only be **weaker** by the time they get to you, but you will also experience **fewer hours of daylight**. So the days will feel **colder** and it will get **dark** earlier.

We call this period of time **winter**, and for us here in the Northern Hemisphere it occurs from December to February. In the depths of winter, the North Pole is in **constant darkness**.

Now, **Uranus** is a weird planet in many ways, but especially when it comes to its spin. Uranus is tilted on its axis **far more** than Earth. In fact it's lying almost on its side, sort of **rolling along** like a ball, at the same time as it travels around the sun. This makes the **differences between the seasons** rather more **exaggerated** than they are on Earth. In fact, if you were standing at one of Uranus's poles (not that you could, you'd sink) you'd be **directly facing the sun** for around a quarter of Uranus's orbit, and during this entire time you would be in **constant daylight.** If you stayed in the same position, you'd end up facing directly **away** from the sun for the opposite quarter, and it would be dark **the entire time.**

Now Uranus is **so far away** from the sun that it has a ridiculously **large orbit** and also experiences far **less** gravitational pull toward the sun than the other planets—except of course poor far-flung Neptune. So not only does Uranus travel **super slowly** but it also has huge **distances** to cover. This means it has a **mega** long orbit time. In fact, a year on Uranus takes an epic 84 Earth-years. And due to its unique sideways tilt, for a quarter of this time one pole is in complete darkness. This would be a madness-inducing **21 years of darkness**. Unless of course you're a mole. In which case you'd be fine.

THE **ANSWER** is **C** ON PARTS OF URANUS IT STAYS DARK FOR 21 YEARS AT A TIME.

NOW, SPEAKING OF DARK PLACES . . .

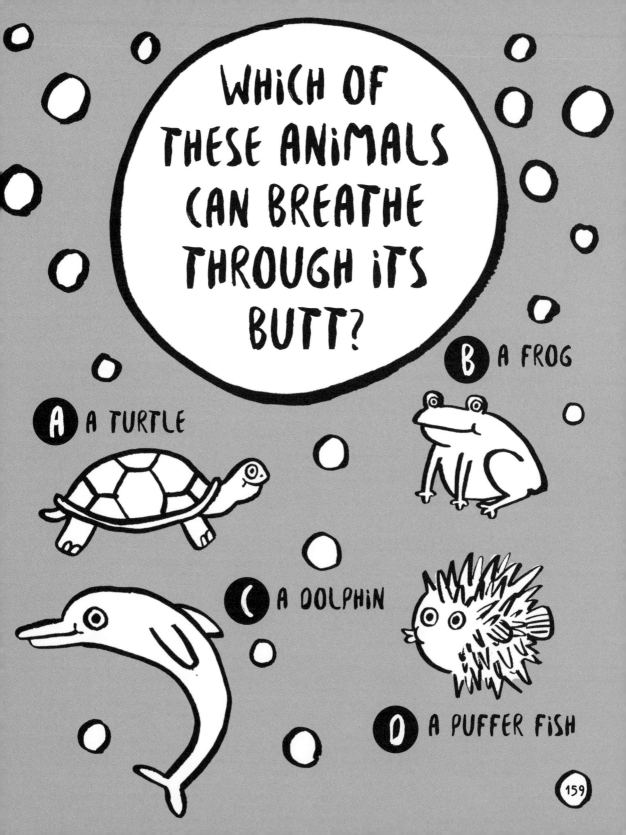

All living creatures need **oxygen** to survive, but you'd have to be rather desperate to get it by breathing through **your butt**, right? I mean, in an ideal world it's not exactly where I'd like to exhale from. Mine, not yours. Well, I wouldn't really like to breathe through your butt either. No offense.

However, there are some brave creatures that use **butt-breathing** on a regular basis, despite the fact that they have a **perfectly good mouth**—and a set of **lungs**. So why not use **them** then, like any sensible person (I mean animal) would? Well, it's pretty **hard** to breathe with your mouth and lungs if you're stuck **underwater** for long periods of time.

So what animals spend a lot of their time underwater? Fish, obviously. But fish use their **gills** to obtain oxygen—special little flaps of skin that **absorb oxygen directly from water** as it flows across them.

How about **dolphins?** Dolphins are **mammals**, which means they **breathe in air** and absorb oxygen from it using their **lungs**. Most dolphins can stay underwater for up to 8-10 minutes but then they have to rise to the surface to suck in fresh air through their **blowhole**—the little hole on the top of their back. That is, once they've blown any old air, along with any stray water, out of it. You might want to steer clear when they do this—this turbo-charged **dolphin snot** can shoot out at up to **100 miles per hour!**

What about **whales** then? Sperm whales can stay underwater for up to a whopping **90 minutes**, thanks to special electrically charged proteins that help their blood carry **high levels of oxygen**, so they don't need to take in air as often. Pretty impressive when you consider that the longest that a human has held their breath underwater is a measly **24 minutes**: a record set in 2016 by a Spanish freediver. But even whales do still have to come up for air **eventually**. That's why **whale watching** is so exciting. You never know when old spermie is going to pop up to the surface . . . but you know he'll have to at some point!

How about frogs? Frogs, like most amphibians, have lungs for breathing when they're on **land**, but also a special type of **skin** that they can use to absorb oxygen when they're underwater—kind of like one **giant gill**. No need for any butt-breathing for them.

But what about if you're an animal that needs to spend a **long time** underwater and you don't have gills like a fish, a blowhole like a dolphin, or special skin like a frog? Sometimes your **butt** is your only hope.

And that's exactly what certain types of **turtle** have to do. Like frogs, turtles have mouths and lungs, which they use for breathing when they're on land. However, the **Australian Fitzroy river turtle** and the **North American eastern painted turtle** spend up to **five months** at a time hibernating in **ice-covered** water to avoid the freezing cold winters on land. Their skin is covered with **thick scales** and a **hard shell**—so they can't do **skin-breathing** like their froggy friends. So they've had to come up with an alternative way to get oxygen when snoozing underwater . . . you guessed it! Their butt.

Now, a turtle's butt isn't exactly a butt like you and I have. Turtles have a sort of **multi-purpose hole** at their rear end called a **cloaca**, through which they urinate, excrete waste, and lay eggs. But it turns out that some turtles when they're underwater can also use it to **absorb oxygen**. The cloaca has two sacs next to it called **bursae**, which can easily **expand** and are lined with **blood vessels**.

The turtle **sucks water in** through its cloaca and into its bursae, where life-giving oxygen can be **absorbed** from the water straight into the turtle's blood vessels. This is similar to how a fish absorbs oxygen across its gills. Then the turtle **shoots** the water back out of its butt (sorry, cloaca) . . . and starts again. Turtles can do this up to **60 times a minute**, and it takes very little energy to do so.

Okay, so this butt-sucking technique isn't strictly-speaking "breathing" (as it doesn't involve air entering their lungs), but it is a very **efficient** way for turtles to get oxygen when there's no air available. This means that they can **hibernate underwater** for long periods of time during the freezing winter without having to come up for air.

THE <u>ANSWER</u> is <u>A</u>
TURTLES CAN "BREATHE" THROUGH THEIR BUTTS.

Turtles are not the only creatures that butt-breathe to stay alive. Some other **potty-puffers** have taken things to a whole new level, finding extraordinary additional uses for their rear-end water-shooting skills. In times of emergency, **baby dragonflies** shoot water out of their cloaca to propel themselves forward so they can escape from predators like **ducks**. Kind of like a turbo-charged water fart. **Sea cucumbers** not only eject water out of their rear ends but also **expel** some of their **insides** with it. The resulting tangly mess of **sticky tubes** can trap a predator that is trying to sneak up on Mr. Cucumber from behind.

Talking of **water farts** . . . manatees, sometimes known as **sea cows**, use underwater farts for a rather different purpose: to control their **position** in the water. Manatees are strange-looking creatures who, according to legend, used to be mistaken for **mermaids**. They gorge on plants all day, which break down in their guts to form enormous quantities of **methane gas**.

The methane builds up in their intestines and then, when it chooses to, the manatee lets out a **giant fart**, expelling some of the trapped gas from its butt as a **stream of bubbles**. The sort of bubbles you might see if you fart in the bath. Not exactly very ladylike behavior for a mermaid.

But the clever thing is that this loss of gas from the manatee's intestines causes the creature to become **less buoyant** so it now **sinks** lower down in the water. Kind of like letting some air out of a life preserver.

If the manatee wants to **rise** a little toward the water's surface, all it has to do is **hold its farts in** for a while and wait for the gas from its lunch to **build up** in its intestines. Easy. As its intestines fill with air, the swollen-bellied manatee becomes more buoyant and rises upward. Like blowing more air into the life preserver. Or taking a **deep breath** while you're lying in the bath.

Sea cows might be clever farters, but in terms of pure fart volume they can't beat the farting prowess of a **domestic** cow.

MORE ABOUT THAT IN A BIT. BUT FIRST, HOW FARTY A FARTER ARE YOU?

167

You know your **annoying** big sister, the one who keeps hogging the TV remote control and making you watch *The Bachelor*? Well, wouldn't it be cool if you could **blow her up** with one of your farts? Could that actually be possible?!

Farting is something we all do. Yes, even your granny lets one rip occasionally. **Everyone farts**. Even Meghan Markle lets one sparkle. The average person lets out **10 to 20 butt stinkers** a day—some of us are just a bit better at **hiding** it than others.

FASCINATING AROMA!

Farting may seem rather silly—not to mention downright embarrassing when your **trouser trumpet** goes off in the middle of the school choir concert. But our farts are totally **essential**. There are even scientists who study farts—they're called **flatologists**.

Every time you eat or drink something you will probably swallow down some **gulps of air** with your food. Plus, there are tiny **bacteria** living in your gut which help to break down your food—and they release some of their own gases too. Without the expulsion of all this **extra gas** from your nether regions, along with the occasional **burp** to lend a helping hand, you'd blow up like a balloon and **explode.** Breaking wind is so important that apparently in ancient Rome, Emperor Claudius passed a **law** stating that it was okay to fart at banquets. It's even been rumored that in South America there's a tribe who fart as **greeting!**

HELLO!

But could all this wasted gas be used to make a whopping great **fart bomb?** Now, this might sound like a bit of a strange idea, but there are rumors on the internet that if you were to fart constantly for **6 years and 9 months** you'd produce enough **flammable gas** to fuel an explosion as mighty as an **atomic bomb.** This has always sounded more than a little bit **ridiculous** to me, so I thought I'd give it a try. Not **literally.** I really don't have that kind of time on my hands. Or the tooting talent. But why don't we try and figure out if it could, **in theory**, be true?

Okay, so where do we begin?

Well, an average Windy-Wendy like you or me (yes, I'm aware that probably neither of us is named Wendy—if you are, let out a cheer please) produces around **17 ounces** of fart gas every day—that's enough to fill a small plastic water bottle with some nice **farty goodness**. Now if we divide this daily fart volume by an average of 14 farts a day, we get about **1.2 ounces of gas** per fart.

17 OZ / 14 FARTS ≈ 1.2 OZ PER FART

IF WE ASSUME THAT A SINGLE FART TAKES ABOUT 1 SECOND, IF YOU WERE TO BREAK WIND CONTINUOUSLY FOR A WHOLE YEAR YOU COULD IN THEORY PRODUCE AROUND A WHOPPING 300,000 GALLONS OF FART GAS.

1.2 OZ X 60 SECS X 60 MINS X 24 HOURS X 365 DAYS = 37,843,200 OZ (= ABOUT 300,000 GALLONS)

Now, there's no way on earth you'd actually be **capable** of producing enough gas to do that. And even if you could, you'd be pretty **exhausted**. And possibly inside out. But let's ignore these minor details and continue.

Okay, so how much **energy** could this amount of fart gas produce? Well, farts are made up of mainly **nitrogen and oxygen** from the **air** we've gulped in while eating and drinking, plus a fair amount of **hydrogen** and **carbon dioxide** produced by the **bacteria** in our guts, and sometimes some **methane** too. Out of these gases, hydrogen and methane are both **flammable.** This means that you can set fire to them and they will release **energy.** Gases like this are called **fuels**, and fuels ... can cause **explosions**.

So how big an explosion could we get from our year's worth of **fart gas?** Well there's not very much **methane** in farts, and methane isn't a very good fuel anyway, so we might as well ignore it—sorry, methane. But there's plenty of **hydrogen**, which is super flammable—so much so that it can be used to power **space rockets**. Now, if we assume that there's about **20 percent** hydrogen present in every fart, then our nearly 300,000 gallons of fart gas might contain around **60,000 gallons** of hydrogen.

300,000 GALLONS OF FART GAS X 20/100 = 60,000 GALLONS OF HYDROGEN

For every gallon of hydrogen that burns, **3 kilojoules of energy** is released. So if we **lit** the hydrogen resulting from our fart-full year, assuming it was mixed with enough air to allow it to **burn fully**, we could release a whopping great **180 thousand kilojoules** of energy.

60,000 GALLONS X 3 KJ = 180,000 KJ

That's an awful lot of energy. To **blow up a small car** requires around 4,000 kJ of energy. With our fart-year's worth of hydrogen we could blow up more than **45 old jaloples**. In fact the explosion produced would be the equivalent of lighting around **1500 lbs** of TNT. That could cause a pretty mega explosion. A **Tomahawk cruise missile**, used in ship-based land-attacks, is equivalent to only **1100 lbs** of TNT. So according to our (somewhat ridiculous) theory, we could easily **fart out** one of those in a year. However, a block of TNT on **Minecraft** contains a whopping great **3600 lbs** of TNT. You'd need nearly 2.5 years of **constant farting** for that!

So how long would you have to fart to produce an explosion with the kind of energy of an **atomic bomb?** The terrible nuclear bomb that was released over Hiroshima during World War II, causing widespread and catastrophic damage, exploded with around **65,000 million kJ** of energy. According to my calculations, you'd have to fart continuously for around **361,000 years** to do that sort of damage.

65,000 MILLION KJ / 180,000 KJ PER YEAR ≈ 361,000 YEARS

So we've shown pretty conclusively that you won't be able to **blow up** your TV-hogging big sister with a fart. But you can always try **stinking** her away.

We all know that farts can be pretty **whiffy**, and that's due to the presence of a tiny amount of **sulfur** in the fart gas, which gives off a rather horrid smell. By the way, if you actually **like** the aroma of a good old stinker (you weirdo) you could always put your nose to good use—and get a job as a **professional fart-smeller**. Seriously, according to ancient Chinese medicine, the precise smell of a person's fart might indicate if they have certain **diseases** . . .

i HAVE BEEN WRONGLY ACCUSED!

SO iN CHINA, EXPERT FART-SNiFFERS HAVE BEEN REPORTED TO GET PAiD UP TO $50,000 A YEAR. YEP, TO SMELL PEOPLE'S FARTS.

Anyway, assuming your sis doesn't actually **enjoy** the smell of a fart, you might be able to use one to expel her from the living room.

To create an eye-watering **tooting-triumph** that would be potent enough to send her **running for the hills** in horror, it might help to eat foods rich in sulfur-like beans, cabbage, cheese, or eggs. Try it. Eat a big cheesy-beans-on-toast with a dollop of cabbage on the side and a boiled egg . . . and then **let one rip**. Your sis will probably run to her room **gasping** for air. And you'll be left king of the couch-castle, brandishing the TV remote with glee. Just don't forget to blame the dog.

YOUR EGGY FART MIGHT BE TRULY STINKY, BUT WHEN IT COMES TO IMPRESSIVE FLATULENCE, VIRTUALLY NOTHING COMPARES TO ONE OF THE MOST PROLIFIC WIND-RELEASERS AROUND . . . THE HUMBLE COW.

MOOOO!

Cows belong to a group of animals called **ruminants,** which also includes sheep, deer, and giraffes. Ruminants have a special stomach called a **rumen**, which contains **bacteria** to help the cow break down tough and coarse food, like grass. In fact, a cow has **four different stomachs**. One for grass, one for ice cream . . . no, I'm joking about the ice cream.

When a cow takes a mouthful of grass, she first gives it a tiny bit of a chew, just enough to be able to **swallow it**, and then she gulps it down into her **first and second stomachs**, the **rumen** and **reticulum**. Here the bacteria go to work on the grass, using a process called **fermentation**. Fermentation releases **methane**. More about this in a minute.

The cow then **regurgitates** her partly digested food (basically she **throws it up** into her mouth, nice) and chews on it a little bit more fully. This is called **chewing the cud**—and is why cows often look like they're chewing gum. After a while our moo-friend swallows the ball of mush down into her third and fourth stomachs, the **omasum** and **abomasum**, where the remainder of the grassy goodness gets fully digested and the **nutrients** are **absorbed** into her bloodstream.

By this time, the hard-working bacteria in her rumen have produced a whole load of **methane gas**, which poor old cowy then has to **get rid of**. The average cow releases a staggering **60 gallons** of methane a day, the vast majority of which comes out of her body in **burps**, and the rest in her **farts** and **poop**. That's more than **1,000 times** the amount of methane released by even the fartiest human, and is enough to fill more than **15 party balloons.**

THE **ANSWER** IS <u>B</u>

EVERY DAY A SINGLE COW BURPS AND FARTS ENOUGH METHANE TO FILL MORE THAN 15 PARTY BALLOONS.

Now, parties aside, here's the thing. There are around **1.5 billion cows** on the planet. Each one burping and farting out 60 gallons of methane every day. Over the course of a year that's more than 32 trillion gallons of methane. **That's an awful lot of methane!**

60 GALLONS X 365 DAYS X 1.5 BILLION COWS = 32,850,000,000,000 GALLONS OF METHANE

Apart from causing some rather **smelly farmyards**, the problem is that methane is what's known as a **greenhouse gas**. You might have heard of this term—we hear it a lot when people talk about **carbon dioxide**, which is another greenhouse gas. Greenhouse gases form a layer around the earth and act like a **snuggly blanket**, trapping the heat from the sun and keeping us warm.

This is mostly a **good** thing—without greenhouse gases in our atmosphere, it would be too **cold** at night for us to survive. However, over the past 100 years or so, a lot more greenhouse gases have been released into our **atmosphere** due to an increase in **human activities** such as **burning fossil fuels**, like oil and gas.

This means that our **snuggly blanket** has been getting slowly **thicker**, causing the earth to **warm up**. This is known as **global warming**, and is having a **serious impact** on our **weather** and on the survival of many **plant** and **animal** species. It is crucial that we all **now work together** to **reduce** the amount of greenhouse gases we release into the atmosphere in an attempt to stop **climate change** and **biodiversity loss** brought about by global warming.

Now, **methane** is not as common a greenhouse gas as carbon dioxide, but the problem is it's much **much better** at **trapping heat** from the sun. In fact, some researchers say that the increase in methane from all the burps, farts, and poop of animals such as cows is having more effect on **global warming** than all the carbon dioxide produced by cars, trains, and planes. So as well as **using fewer fossil fuels**, you can do your bit to combat climate change by **eating less beef and dairy**.

IN THE FUTURE WE'LL PROBABLY ALL BE EATING INSECTS ANYWAY. TRUE THAT. THEY'RE A GREAT SOURCE OF PROTEIN. AND PRETTY TASTY.

While cow burps are definitely a problem, most of the methane in our atmosphere comes from **naturally decaying dead material** in wetlands, rivers, and streams.

WEIRDLY THOUGH, IT'S BEEN FOUND THAT SEA CREATURES SUCH AS MUSSELS, OYSTERS, AND CLAMS ALSO GIVE OFF LOTS OF METHANE—ALTHOUGH NOT AS MUCH AS COWS. PERHAPS WE SHOULD TELL THEM NOT TO BE SO SHELLFISH? HAHA.

But, believe it or not, it's thought that the most **prolific** living methane producer is a tiny creature called a **termite**. Termites are ant-like insects that play an important role in **breaking down dead wood**, returning the **nutrients** from the **wood** to the soil. But they can also be a right old pain if you live in a wooden house. If termites are so tiny, I hear you cry, surely they can only produce really small amounts of methane? Yes. The trouble is, there are around **1 million billion** of them on the planet! It's thought that together these tiny terrors produce up to **150 million tons** of methane a year.

THE OTHER WEIRD THING ABOUT TERMITES IS THAT THEY FIND A RATHER INTERESTING USE FOR THEIR POOP . . .

A BUILDING A HOUSE OUT OF IT

B MAKING A SUNSHADE OUT OF IT

C THROWING IT AT THEIR PREDATORS

WHICH OF THESE IS **NOT** A REAL WAY THAT AN ANIMAL MAKES USE OF ITS POOP?

D USING IT AS A DISGUISE

Terrible termites are estimated to cause around 1 billion dollars of **damage** in the United States each year. These tiny ant-like terrorists wreak havoc, **nibbling away** at your mom's new wooden boat or your grandma's antique coffee table. So, understandably, people are constantly trying to **get rid of them**. But the trouble is, these little critters seem to have superhuman powers of **survival**. Not only are they able to survive infections from the sort of **dangerous bacteria** that usually kill other small insects, but they also put up a valiant fight against many of the **pesticides** that we humans spray on them to try to get rid of them.

So how come termites are so **tough?** Well, it all seems to be down to their **protective houses**. Sorry, nests. You see termites build their nests out of . . . you guessed it! **POOP**. (Strictly speaking, a mixture of poop and dead wood.) But poop isn't exactly **strong**, so how does this protective **poop-home** help them to survive? Well, it seems that the poop provides a yummy **feeding place** for certain types of **friendly bacteria**, who live in the poop-fortress walls. The grateful bugs **repay the favor** by releasing **nasty chemicals** that kill the termites' enemies!

UNLiKE TERMiTES AND THEiR PROTECTiVE POOP, SKiPPER CATERPiLLARS USE **POOP-THROWiNG** TO CONFUSE THEiR PREDATORS.

Hiding safely out of sight, a little skipper caterpillar steadily increases the **blood pressure** in its butt—and then suddenly lets rip, firing **poop-missiles** high into the air. These little poop decoys can land up to several yards away—a throwing-distance more than **40 times** skippie's body length. That's the equivalent of you lobbing a piece of your poop nearly from one end of a **football field** to the other—using only your **butt**. Pretty impressive. I dare you to try that next time you're at practice.

When wasps and other **predators** arrive on the scene, they excitedly follow the **caterpillar-poop trail**, expecting to find their multi-legged pooper prey nearby. But of course the sneaky skipper is **nowhere to be found**. While butt-catapulting might work for caterpillars, it's probably not a good idea to use this poop-slinging technique to confuse your **mom** next time she comes looking for you to **wash the dishes**.

Some animals have found another sneaky way to confuse their predators—by **disguising themselves as poop**. The orb weaver spider, giant swallowtail caterpillar, and pied warty frog all **impersonate bird poop** to protect themselves from getting eaten. Seems pretty sensible. I wouldn't want to eat bird poop, **would you?!** Google some photos of them. They look pretty poopy.

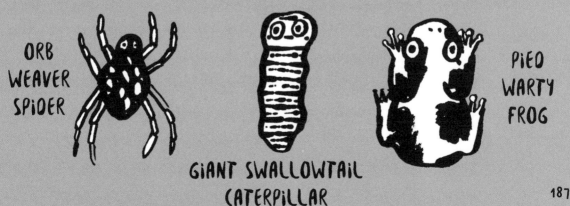

ORB WEAVER SPIDER

GIANT SWALLOWTAIL CATERPILLAR

PIED WARTY FROG

So that leaves the only option for something that poop **can't** be used for as . . . making a sunshade. Well, I certainly don't know of any animals that can do that. **Do you?**

Although of course this doesn't mean it's **impossible**. What I **do** know is that if you're lying on a tropical beach in the Caribbean, your **sunshade** may not be made out of poop . . . but the **beach** probably is! **Parrotfish poop**, to be precise. Parrotfish have huge **horse-like**

teeth that they use to **grind** up **coral**, in search of any yummy green **algae** living within it. The coral waste then passes through the fish's body and gets **pooped** out . . . and washes ashore as beautiful white **sand**. A single parrotfish can produce nearly **220 lbs** of sand in a year! That's enough sand to fill a small sandpit.

THE **ANSWER** is **B**
MAKING A SUNSHADE OUT OF POOP IS **NOT** A REAL WAY THAT AN ANIMAL MAKES USE OF ITS POOP.

SO, IT APPEARS THAT ANIMALS HAVE A WHOLE ARRAY OF STRANGE USES FOR THEIR BUTT EXCRETIONS. BUT SOMETIMES EVEN WE HUMANS CAN FIND A USE FOR AN ANIMAL'S POOP . . .

A A PRAIRIE DOG

B A CIVET CAT

C A DESERT RAT

D A GUINEA PIG

COFFEE TASTES BETTER WHEN THE COFFEE BEANS HAVE BEEN POOPED OUT OF WHICH ANIMAL?

189

Your mom probably likes a nice cup of **coffee** with her breakfast in the morning. So do most people. In fact, in the US we drink a turbo-charged **400 million cups** of the stuff a day. That's enough to fill 38 Olympic-sized swimming pools. If you **drank** all that coffee you might even be able to **swim** across all of them in one try. Although I wouldn't recommend it. You'd only turn your nice white bathing suit all brown.

Anyway, how do you think your mom would feel if you told her that, as a special Mother's Day treat, you'd taken some of her **favorite coffee beans**, fed them to the **cat**, collected the **stinky remnants** from the litter box . . . then turned them into the **steaming mug** of murky brown stuff she's happily sipping away at? She'd probably **splutter** it all over you in horror, **right?**

Well, in Indonesia there is a type of animal called a **civet cat.** While she might look a bit like a pointy-faced cat, the Asian palm civet is not actually strictly speaking a cat. This fearless feline-like forager can **climb trees** . . . and while she's pottering around up there she munches on little berries called **coffee cherries.** A coffee cherry is basically a hard coffee bean surrounded by sweet fleshy fruit. Kinda like a cherry. Hence the name. Obvs.

Now, unlike us humans, once the crazy cat has taken a few bites from the juicy cherry, she **swallows the rest down whole.** No spitting the pits out into grandma's flowerbed.

191

Once swallowed, the **half-nibbled** coffee-cherry works its way down into the cat's stomach and intestines, where chemicals called **enzymes** go to work on it, breaking down all the **yummy fruit** into smaller substances such as **sugars**.

This process is called **digestion**. The sugars are then **absorbed** into the cat's **bloodstream** and carried around its body to its cells. Here, the sugars can be **stored** or **broken down further** to provide the civet cat with **energy**—so it can run up another tree and start the munching process all over again. This is just the same as how digestion works in us humans.

Once the fruity part of the cherry has been digested in this way, this leaves behind the **hard coffee bean**—which continues working its way down through the rest of the cat's **digestive system**. Eventually the hard bean **pops** out of the cat's body . . . yep, in its poop.

Now here's the **disgusting** bit. Farmers come along and **gather up** the bean-filled civet poop, get rid of the, er, poopy bits, and then they **collect the beans**. And these beans are then roasted, ground up . . . and used to make coffee.

According to many people, this **civet coffee** made from the pooped out beans—known in Indonesia as **kopi luwak**—tastes simply **delicious**. It's thought this could be because the fussy civet selects only the **best** and **ripest** coffee cherries to eat. Or because the enzymes in the cat's digestive system change the structure of the **proteins** in the bean, reducing the **acidity** and making the resulting coffee taste **smoother**. Some experts even say that as the bean passes out of the civet cat's butt, the bean takes on a **"musky smoothness"** that you can later taste in the coffee.

> HMM. i WONDER HOW THEY GET THE BEANS OUT OF THE POOP. PERHAPS THEY . . . SiEVE iT? HA HA GET iT? SiEVE-iT? CiVET? OH OKAY, i GiVE UP.

Anyway, whatever the reason for its apparently delicious taste, kopi luwak has become one of the most sought-after and **expensive** coffees in the world.

> MMMMM! DELiCiOUS!

> iN FACT, iN THE UNiTED STATES, A SiNGLE CUP OF THE STUFF CAN COST YOU UP TO 80 DOLLARS!

THE **ANSWER** is **B**

COFFEE TASTES BETTER WHEN THE COFFEE BEANS HAVE BEEN POOPED OUT OF A CIVET CAT.

JUST TO BE CLEAR, THIS WON'T WORK WITH YOUR MOM'S CAT. EVEN IF YOU FED HER COFFEE BEANS FOR DINNER. THE CAT, NOT YOUR MOM. ALTHOUGH THAT WON'T WORK EITHER. SO DON'T BOTHER.

On a serious note, before you rush over to Bali (or a posh coffee shop) to try and get hold of some kopi luwak, please **be careful**. There are farmers out there who have taken advantage of this **booming demand** for pooped-out coffee beans and are really not very **kind** to the poor old civet cats—keeping them in **terrible conditions** and **force-feeding** them coffee cherries in an attempt to try to get them to produce loads of bean-filled poop. Buying civet coffee from these farmers only **encourages** this cruel behavior. The problem is it's pretty hard to tell whether a bag of kopi luwak coffee was made from **wild** or **caged** civets, no matter what the label says. So it might be safest just to avoid it. Sorry.

EITHER WAY, YOU CAN STILL DISGUST YOUR FRIENDS BY TELLING THEM THAT THERE ARE PEOPLE OUT THERE WHO DRINK COFFEE MADE FROM A CIVET CAT'S BEAN-PACKED BUTT-EXCRETIONS.

But if you think **that's** disgusting, there's an animal that **eats** butt excretions. Yes really. Not the butt-excretions of a civet cat, but **its own butt excretions**. And for rather good reasons too. Can you guess what it is?

WHICH REVOLTING ANIMAL REGULARLY EATS ITS OWN POOP?

A — A DOG

B — A MONKEY

C — A RABBIT

D — A BEETLE

YOU might have noticed that your pet dog takes an occasional **poop-snack** when it goes out on its evening prowl. Indeed, many of us have seen perfectly polite canines having a good old **sniff** at, and even an odd **nibble** on, other doggies' stinky doo-doos. And sometimes even on their own. Ewwww! Imagine eating your own poop?! No. Thank. You.

But for a dog, this actually makes good sense. You see, occasionally there's a tiny bit of **undigested food** left behind in a dog's stinky poop. Especially if the dog has been **wolfing** its food down in a hurry. So, having a bit of a munch on it might sound **revolting**, but it can actually be quite **nutritious** for the stinky-mouthed mutt. In fact, monkeys do the same thing too. But, like dogs, **not very often.**

Dung beetles also feed off the nutrients in poop. But it's the poop from **other** creatures, not their own. They even have special mouthparts to **slurp** up the runny bits. Nice. Some even make **houses** in the poop, or use it as a nice soft place to lay their **eggs**. A bit like a poop nursery.

However, the absolute **king** of self-excretion-eating is none other than . . . yep, you guessed it! A **rabbit.** Have you ever seen your friend's cute pet bunny **licking its own butt?** Not so cute now, eh?!

Rabbits, like some other small animals such as guinea pigs, have **very short guts** so they simply don't have **time** to digest all their food the **first time** it passes through their body. This means that their first poop-attempts contain lots of valuable **nutrients** that the rabbit's body didn't manage to get hold of.

So the rabbit **gobbles up** these soft, fresh poop pellets—the ones that look all dark and mushy—as soon as they pop out of its butt . . . and it has another go at digesting them.

Then the whole thing happens **again**. It's thought that this **poop-eating process** can take place up to **12 times** before the final dry, round **droppings**, stripped of all possible nutrients, get left behind.

Please don't try this at home. It absolutely doesn't work for humans. And you'll most likely get very sick. And, useful or not, I can't imagine eating your own butt-goo tastes terribly good.

THE **ANSWER** is (

A RABBIT REGULARLY EATS ITS OWN POOP.

BUT SPEAKING OF THINGS THAT TASTE GOOD, WHAT DO YOU RECKON THE CENTER OF OUR GALAXY TASTES LIKE?

197

The center of a Milky Way probably does indeed taste like chocolate (ha ha, see what I did there?). However, the center of **the** Milky Way, as in, **our galaxy**, is most likely to taste like . . . something rather different.

If you were to travel at the **speed of light** for **26,000 years** in the right direction, you'd probably get to the **center** of the Milky Way. That's like traveling in a fast car for around **300 billion years**. And if, when your 300 billion-year-old body got there, you were able to take off your space helmet and **breathe in** the mix of chemicals swirling around you . . . and **if** you were able to **survive** for more than a few moments in the absence of any life-giving **oxygen** (unlikely) . . .

. . . **If** you managed all of that, then you **might just** open up your 300-billion-year old mouth nice and wide and breathe in a **glorious scent**. A scent so strong it might be almost as if you could **taste** it. The fabulous mouth-watering scent of . . . **ethyl formate**. Oh.

This rather boring-sounding chemical happens to be one of a large number of chemicals that were recently identified in a **dust cloud** called **Sagittarius B2**, which lies close to the center of the Milky Way. This dust cloud was studied using a clever device called a **radio telescope**, which can be used to "look at" things we can't actually **see**, as it detects **radio waves** instead of light. Kinda like how a **night vision camera** works by detecting **infrared rays**.

Now, ethyl formate is about the same size as a simple **amino acid.** And amino acids, which come together to form **proteins**, are the **building blocks of life**. So the discovery of this amino-acid-sized chemical out there in the depths of space helps to support the idea that **alien life** just **might** be possible.

BUT BY FAR THE MOST INTERESTING THING ABOUT ETHYL FORMATE IS THAT IT HAPPENS TO BE THE MAIN FLAVOR IN . . . WAIT FOR IT . . . RASPBERRIES.

Raspberries might not be the only thing you'd come back smelling of if you took a quick **stroll** in outer space. Some astronauts, on welcoming their spacewalking buddies back onto their ship, have claimed that their space suits smell sort of **sweet** and **metallic,** a bit like the fumes from a **steam engine**. Some have even said it was like the smell of **charred steak.**

They're probably smelling chemicals called **polycyclic aromatic hydrocarbons**. Yeah, easy for you to say. These chemicals are formed by the **burning** that occurs when **stars die,** and they stick to **fibers** like clothing. Kinda like how your sweater smells of **wood smoke** for days after you've been sitting around a **campfire.**

THE **ANSWER** is **A**
THE CENTER OF OUR GALAXY PROBABLY TASTES LIKE RASPBERRIES.

BIZARRELY, SIMILAR CHEMICALS HAPPEN TO BE FOUND IN BACON. SO IF YOU EVER GET TO MEET THE BRITISH ASTRONAUT TIM PEAKE, GIVE HIS CLOTHES A QUICK DISCREET SNIFF AND SEE IF HE SMELLS LIKE A BACON SANDWICH. THEN EAT THEM FOR BREAKFAST WITH A NICE GLASS OF MILK. SPEAKING OF MILK . . .

WHAT KIND OF COWS MIGHT PRODUCE THE MOST MILK?

A COWS THAT DRINK WATER ALL DAY

B COWS THAT SIT DOWN ALL DAY

C COWS WITH NAMES

D COWS WITH BLUE EYES

Most of us like a nice splash of **milk** on our breakfast in the morning. Unless you have **toast**. Milk on toast would just be **weird**.

These days, people drink all kinds of weird and wonderful milk—soy milk, almond milk, coconut milk, goat's milk. I tried camel milk once. **Bleurgh**. I can't say I was a fan. Humph.

SUIT YOURSELF!

There are even people out there who drink **reindeer milk**. Reindeer produce milk with one of the highest amounts of **fat** of all the milks drunk by humans—being nearly **¼ fat**. Great if you're a chilly baby reindeer needing **snuggly warmth** in the snow, but no wonder Santa has such a **big tummy**. Whale milk is a whopping **50 per cent fat**, but as far as I know no one other than **whale calves** drinks that.

The most **commonly** drunk milk is still, of course, good old **cow's milk**. The problem is, with about **1,070 cups a year** drunk by each person in the US, this puts a **huge demand** on farmers to rear as many **cows** as they can to produce **enough milk** to keep our supermarket shelves topped up.

So, many farmers try to rear their cows in such a way that each cow produces **as much milk as possible**. In fact there are over **250 million** milk-producing cows across the world, with some cows producing up to **16 gallons** of the stuff a day.

USING ONE SUCH COW, YOU COULD FILL THE GAS TANK OF YOUR MOM'S CAR WITH MILKY GOODNESS. BUT DON'T DO THAT. YOU WON'T GET VERY FAR.

Sadly, to increase milk production to these sorts of levels, farmers often keep cows under **terrible conditions** and treat them pretty **unkindly**. So wouldn't it be great if we could find **new ways** to produce more milk, without being cruel to the poor old cows?

Well, let's look at some of my proposed answers to this question to see if we could **help matters**. Firstly, milk consists mostly of **water,** so it would indeed make **sense** that the more water a cow drinks, the more milk she might produce. But in fact, unless a cow is pretty **dehydrated**, drinking more water is pretty unlikely to have any effect on her milk. She will just **pee** more. Like **you** would if you drank 15 cups of water at recess. So, sadly, this simple-sounding solution **won't help much**.

Okay, so what about **sitting down** all day? Well, apart from water, milk also contains **sugars** and **proteins** dissolved in the water, and tiny droplets of **fat** floating about in it, forming an **emulsion**. Some of these fat droplets get **skimmed off** the top of the milk before it's sold, to make **semi-skimmed** or even **skimmed** milk, which contain **less fat** than **full-fat** milk. Bizarrely, in New Zealand there was once a cow called Marge who had a defect in one of her **genes** that meant that she

naturally produced **less fat** in her milk. Marge has since been used to breed . . . **semi-skimmed cows!** There's also a breed of cows that produce **milkshakes**. Seriously, they **dance** all day.

OKAY, SO MAYBE THAT PART'S NOT TRUE.

Anyway, back to the point. To produce substances like fats and sugars in their milk, cows need **energy**. Just like we need energy to help us **grow**. Like us, cows get energy from the **food** that they eat. Now, if a cow **sits down and eats grass** all day, she's not using much of her energy for running around (okay, plodding around), so she will have more energy **left over** to do **other** things—like make fat. Or play the piano.

BOOTIFUL MOOSIC

So, given that milk **contains fat,** we might expect cows that sit down all day to produce **more** of it. However, while this makes perfect sense, what actually usually happens is that the cows just get . . . **fat**. Just like you would if you sat in front of the TV all day and ate cake.

SO COULD IT BE THAT COWS WITH **NAMES** PRODUCE MORE MILK? BIZARRELY, THIS RIDICULOUS-SOUNDING ANSWER COULD BE TRUE.

Hi, I'M DAISY

Now this doesn't really have anything to do with the name itself. It's all about how **happy** the cow is. You see, cows with names usually just happen to have a **good relationship** with their farmer; she's nice to them, looks after them well, and treats them as **individuals**. This means that cows with names happen to be happier and more **relaxed**. When cows are stressed they release chemicals called **stress hormones**, just like we humans do, and these chemicals stop the cows from doing anything that isn't really **essential** for survival, such as producing milk. So **happy relaxed cows** produce **fewer stress hormones** . . . and therefore produce **more milk**.

THE **ANSWER** is **C**
COWS WITH NAMES MIGHT PRODUCE MORE MILK.

This is what scientists call **correlation** rather than **causation**. It **doesn't** mean that if you went up to a **random** cow in a **random** field and said "Hello, Daisy!" she would suddenly start producing more milk. That would be causation. And would be quite **ridiculous**. And would make a mess of your shoes.

In fact, **anything** that makes a cow happier and more relaxed is likely to make her produce more milk. Even listening to **music**. Or should I say **moooooosic?** Studies have shown that cows produce more milk when listening to slow, relaxing melodies like **love ballads** or **Beethoven**. Some farmers even play relaxing music to their **chickens** to try to help them lay more eggs!

MOOBY MOOBY MOO

So if you know any farmers, please tell them to be **kind** to their cows. Cows are **sensitive creatures**. In fact, according to some studies, cows have "best friends" and, like us, get stressed when they're **separated** from each other. It's even thought that cows have a range of **personalities** such as **boldness** and **shyness**, and that they vary in how **moody** or **sociable** they are. Some cows even **recognize people**—choosing to stand closer to people who have handled them **gently** in the past.

One thing that might make a cow, or your sister, **even happier** would be to give her a bit of a **tickle**. But did you know that you can **block** a tickle?

209

A TENSE YOUR MUSCLES

B THINK ABOUT SOMETHING ELSE

HOW DO YOU BLOCK A TICKLE?

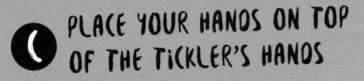

C PLACE YOUR HANDS ON TOP OF THE TICKLER'S HANDS

D HOLD YOUR BREATH AND STICK OUT YOUR TONGUE

Most of us feel **ticklish** on at least some part of our body. But for many of us, while it might make us laugh, the experience of being tickled is not exactly **enjoyable.** Far from it. In fact, some people even have a **tickle phobia.** It's called **pteronophobia.** Although that sounds rather more like a fear of pterodactyls.

TICKLE, TICKLE!

Anyway, wouldn't it be amazing if you could **block** the tickly feelings of a tickle, stopping your **evil tickler** in their tracks? Well, you can. Want to know **how?** Thought you might.

Distracting your brain by focusing on something else might help **a little.** Like the most boringly unfunny thing you can think of. Say, **granny's nightie?** Or the weather forecast. Or the prospect of **tidying your room**. However, if that fails, the absolute **best** way to block a tickle requires us to understand a little about the **brain** and **why** we feel ticklish in the first place.

Have you ever noticed that you **can't tickle yourself?** Try it. Doesn't work, right? You see, for us to feel ticklish, our brain has to be **surprised**. This makes good sense. You see, back in **caveman** days, a surprising feeling on our skin was likely to have been a sneaky little **creature** coming along to bite or sting or scratch us, or even infect us with a **deadly disease**. There weren't any doctors or hospitals back then, so having tickly feelings helped us to **react quickly** to **unexpected** and potentially **dangerous** creatures, causing us to **flick** them away.

While we might have **evolved** a lot since then, like in our ability to eat with a knife and fork and do algebra (although perhaps not at the same time), many of our **survival instincts** still remain the same. And this ancient **survival response** to tickly tormentors occurs in modern-day **animals** too. You might have seen a horse give a good old **shudder** to try and get rid of a tickly fly that's landed on its back, or **flick** the irritating insect off with its tail.

But what if you were to feel ticklish every time **anything** brushed against the tickly parts of your skin, even if it **wasn't a surprise?** You'd fall down laughing every time you put on your shoes and socks! To prevent this, your brain **blocks** the tickly feelings when your **own hands** are doing the tickling. As your hands move toward your body, a part of your brain makes a **prediction** as to exactly how they are going to **feel** on your own skin, which blocks your tickle response.

So when **someone else** tickles you, all you have to do is to **trick** your brain into thinking that it's **your** hands doing the tickling. Simply place your hands **on top** of the evil tickler's hands while they're trying to tickle you. Your brain can now make a pretty good **prediction** as to how their hands will feel on your skin, **as if** they're your own hands. This removes the element of **surprise** . . . and . . . **bingo!** No more tickly feelings.

THE **ANSWER** IS **C**
TO BLOCK A TICKLE, SIMPLY PLACE YOUR HANDS ON TOP OF THE TICKLER'S HANDS.

BY THE WAY, THERE IS ONE PLACE WHERE YOU CAN TICKLE YOURSELF—CAN YOU FIND IT? THE ROOF OF YOUR MOUTH. TRY IT. DID YOU SQUEAL?!

Being ticklish is not just a survival response to protect us from harm. There is a also a rather different type of tickle that exists to make us **laugh**—releasing feel-good hormones such as **oxytocin** that make us feel all **soft** and **squishy**, helping us to **bond** with our tickler. Assuming you actually like them enough to **not mind** being tickled by them.

Interestingly if you tickle your baby sister she **probably won't know it's you** who is tickling her. Until the age of about six months, babies certainly **feel** tickly feelings but they don't realize the feelings are coming from the **outside world**.

So if you tickle her toes she might **gurgle** a bit, but she'll probably just think that her foot has **randomly** started to feel all funny.

Other than us humans, **few animals** are programmed to get this kind of **pleasure** from tickling. It makes sense that chimps, gorillas, and orangutans—being our **closest living relatives**—quite like the odd tickle. But bizarrely, the only other animal that seems to **enjoy** being tickled is . . . **a rat**. When tickled on their backs and bellies,

SQUEAK!

rats not only **jump with glee**, but they even let out high-pitched **squeaks** of pleasure. A sort of ratty giggle. Perhaps we should call it a **riggle?!** And when the tickling stops, the **riggling** rats chase their tickler's hand around their cage, as if begging to be tickled again!

Apart from amusing rats or tormenting your little sister, mastering the **art of tickling** can have its uses. For example if you wanted to catch a **lobster**. Obviously. **Lobster-hunters** in the South Florida waters encourage spiny lobsters out of their holes by **tapping** them gently, just behind their tail, using what's known as a **tickle stick**. The poor unsuspecting lobsters think they're being **attacked** from behind and **scuttle forward,** straight into the fishermen's nets.

THIS iS FUN!

While tickling might be a good way to catch lobsters, and laughter can help **strengthen** our close relationships, please don't go around tickling all your friends **willy-nilly**. Unless, of course, it's to teach them the tickle-block trick. You see, some people really **don't like** being tickled. In fact it can make them feel pretty **scared**. Especially if you're **bigger** and **stronger** than them. Tickling was even used as a form of **torture** during World War II.

So **check in** with your tickle-buddy first, and please **listen** if they say **stop**. It might **look like** they're laughing their head off, but tickling activates a part of the brain that causes **smile-like** movements of the face, even if the person **isn't actually happy**. So, you can't **assume** that they're enjoying it. Weird, eh? No wonder it's a **pain** trying to convince your tickler that you're not really having fun.

SPEAKING OF PAIN, DID YOU KNOW THAT THERE'S A PART OF YOUR BODY THAT CAN'T FEEL ANY PAIN? YES, THAT'S RIGHT. YOU SEE, THE SKIN ON YOUR . . .

WAIT! HANG ON A MINUTE. HAVEN'T WE DONE THIS ONE ALREADY?

YEP, WE HAVE. HA HA, TRICKED YOU! CAN YOU REMEMBER THE ANSWER? AND MORE IMPORTANTLY, CAN YOU REMEMBER **WHY?** DON'T WORRY IF YOU'VE FORGOTTEN, YOU CAN ALWAYS GO RIGHT BACK TO THE BEGINNING OF THIS BOOK . . . AND START ALL OVER AGAIN.

Which means you don't need **me** any more. Yes, I know it's sad, but that's it for me. Thanks for trying to figure out the answers to all these questions with me. Isn't it **amazing** how much **weird** and **wonderful** stuff there is going on in the world around us? But what's even **more** cool is that by asking the **right questions**, and with a little bit of help from **science**, it **all makes sense**. Bing!

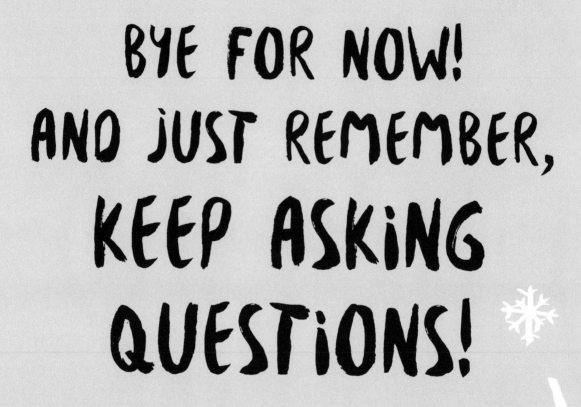

BYE FOR NOW!
AND JUST REMEMBER,
KEEP ASKING
QUESTIONS!

Acknowledgments

Thank you to my dad, Ashley, for a childhood of stories and ideas and a lifetime of explanations. To my mom, Susan, for creative advice, moral support, and believing I could fly. To my step-mom, Debbie, for always being there. To my grandmother Rosemary for inspiring me to write stories. To my six not-so-little-any-more little sisters for keeping me young at heart. To all the kids who've watched my live shows and asked brilliant questions that I'd never have thought to ask. To the team from Duck Quacks Don't Echo, for sourcing some of the facts in this book and helping me believe I have something to say. To Ali, for your beautiful imagination and creative ideas and for putting up with all my stressing during the hatching of this book. To Melody, for helping me get the idea out there. To Zoe Laughlin, for the beautiful artwork accompanying my original pitch, and to my wonderful illustrator, Alice, for bringing it all to life. To my lovely media agent, Jo, for helping me find a publisher, and to my equally lovely literary agent, Stephanie, for taking over the reins and supporting me—thank you both for your generosity and team work. To my publishers, Saskia and Isobel, for getting on board with this baby, believing in me, and trusting me to do it my way. To Isaac, Mercutio, Anna, Luke, Lucy, Osian, and Jude for being my brilliant and inquisitive guinea pigs. To my heart team, Katie, Michelle, Olivia, Fay, and Simon, for holding my hand along this crazy journey. To my partner, Kimwei, for your limitless love, laughter, wisdom, and editorial support. And finally to Nick, my crazy-brained, monster-socked friend, magic-monitor, and accountability-aardvark—I couldn't have done this without you.